What peop   T0167515

Kilimanjaro, Millennial Style

As someone with no interest in adventure travel, I was surprised to find that I couldn't put this book down. The narrative is absorbing and engaging; the story is told with such authenticity that it captured my imagination the way a good novel would, leaving me eager to follow the students' journey and find out what would happen next. Despite being written by a variety of authors, the voice seemed very consistent and the book transitioned smoothly from one chapter to the next. I was completely caught up in the students' thoughts and emotions; I felt as though I was walking alongside them as they faced each challenge, getting to know them, and cheering them on to achieve their goal. I felt fortunate to benefit from the lessons they learned without having to leave the comfort of my warm, safe home. I enthusiastically recommend this book to anyone who might be contemplating a similar trip (or whose child has proposed such a trip) and also to anyone who loves to get lost in a fascinating, compelling, and well-told story.

Dr. Diane Miller, Director of Student Academic Services at the University of Georgia

My husband and I read Dr. Parks' and his students' book as we were preparing to travel to Tanzania and climb Kilimanjaro. We found it very useful—from the practical packing lists, to the personal descriptions of the ecosystems we would travel through as we climbed, to the methods to assess how tour companies treat their porters. We particularly appreciated the "raw truth" that this book conveyed. While we have done our homework and read the standard guidebooks about Kilimanjaro and Tanzania, reading this book was more like having the opportunity to peruse a good friend's journal of her trip. It provided unique and unfiltered perspectives that we had not found in more commercial guidebooks. It was a quick, easy, and fun read, packed with good information. I would definitely recommend this book!

Fellow Faculty Member at the University of Georgia (arranged by Dr. Miller)

Who would sign up for a course that teaches you courage, cooperation, and endurance—how to be stretched to your limits? The 22 'Millennial' authors of this book, that's who! They not only climbed Kilimanjaro together as a class, but then wrote about it together. That's what makes the book truly innovative. Sure, novels often provide the perspectives of many different characters, but I've never before encountered a non-fiction literary travel adventure told from 22 different points of view. Their multiple perspectives create a stunning kaleidoscope through which we experience the dazzling and sometimes harrowing trek to the top of Africa's most iconic peak.

Tim Ward, author of *Zombies on Kilimanjaro*

Kilimanjaro, Millennial Style

The Mountain We Climbed

Kilimanjaro, Millennial Style

The Mountain We Climbed

Edited by Rodney Parks

CHANGEMAKERS
BOOKS

Winchester, UK
Washington, USA

JOHN HUNT PUBLISHING

First published by Changemakers Books, 2022
Changemakers Books is an imprint of John Hunt Publishing Ltd., No. 3 East Street,
Alresford, Hampshire SO24 9EE, UK
office@jhpbooks.com
www.johnhuntpublishing.com
www.changemakers-books.com

For distributor details and how to order please visit the 'Ordering' section on our website.

ISBN: 978 1 78904 957 2
978 1 78904 958 9 (ebook)
Library of Congress Control Number: 2021949609

Design: Matthew Greenfield

UK: Printed and bound by CPI Group (UK) Ltd, Croydon, CR0 4YY
Printed in North America by CPI GPS partners

We operate a distinctive and ethical publishing philosophy in
all areas of our business, from our global network of authors to
production and worldwide distribution.

Contents

The class reaches the Uhuru Peak, 5,895 meters above sea level, the highest freestanding peak in Africa.
Courtesy of the Tanzania Wilderness and Adventure Course

About the Authors

About the 25 student and faculty authors who contributed to this book:

Interdependence and collaboration are essential to accomplish the goal of summiting Mt. Kilimanjaro. In a society that reveres individual accomplishment, climbing Kilimanjaro is an activity that can't be undertaken alone, in which the survival of every group member is dependent on their guides, porters, fellow hikers, and course instructors. Every chapter of this book illustrates vividly the power of this collaboration and the spectacular achievements that are possible by acknowledging and embracing the need for interdependence. This book provides a natural outgrowth of the experiences of the first class of college students at Elon University to take on the challenge of climbing the mountain while telling their story. The student authors constructed a narrative in the same way they undertook this journey: collectively, as a cohesive and interdependent team.

The student authors of this book are: Abby Fuller, Bailey Honig, Carson White, Cole Kocjancic, Daniela Nasser, Dara Sypes, Emma Renfro, Grace Jackson, Jack DiPietro, Junie Burke, Katherine Field, Kenneth Sklar, Konnor Porro, Liam Lindy, Meg Rude, Megan Barber, Morgan Collins, Nathan Jones, Neel Dhanani, Nik Streit, Tim Boles, and Victoria Baumgarten. Faculty authors include University President Dr. Connie Book, Primary Course Instructor Dr. Rodney Parks, Experiential Learning Faculty Dr. Carol Smith, and staff instructors Ms. Kelly Reimer and Ms. Kristen Aquilino. Finally, Dr. Diane Miller and Ms. Abby Fuller provided professional editing of the manuscript.

Acknowledgments

My dearest class, thank you for the memories we made during the inaugural class to hike to the top of Kilimanjaro. I'm eternally grateful to each of you for being flexible and helping me to develop a wonderful class for future learners. Having a group of students write a guidebook for future hikers is a challenging process.

Special thanks to Abby Fuller for being the first person to read, edit, and organize the chapters of the manuscript, a very daunting task. Additionally, many thanks to Dr. Diane Miller, who served as a professional editor and reader of the manuscript. Diane, I can't thank you enough for always being willing to read my work (including my dissertation) and make the necessary suggestions to always strengthen my writing.

To my co-instructors, Kelly Reimer and Kristen Aquilino, I could not have made this class (or this book) happen without you. With each step on the trail you made a difference in the students we serve and I will be forever grateful for your willingness to endure the challenges of teaching the course. And to our Teaching Assistant, Nathan Jones, thank you for your leadership, tenacity, and willingness to push students to deeply engage in the experience.

Finally, to all those that were part of the journey and writing this book: Abby Fuller, Bailey Honig, Carson White, Cole Kocjancic, Daniela Nasser, Dara Sypes, Emma Renfro, Grace Jackson, Jack DiPietro, Junie Burke, Katherine Field, Kenneth Sklar, Konnor Porro, Liam Lindy, Meg Rude, Megan Barber, Morgan Collins, Nathan Jones, Neel Dhanani, Nik Streit, Tim Boles, Victoria Baumgarten, Kristen Aquilino, Kelly Reimer, Dr. Carol Smith, Janelle Papay Decato, and Dr. Connie Book.

Foreword

Dr. Connie Ledoux Book
President, Elon University

The pages that follow chronicle the profound impact of experiential education. Not only is summiting Kilimanjaro—"Kili" to those who come to know the mountain personally—a pinnacle adventure, but the process of preparing for the summit is itself a learning experience of the highest order. Students who prepare for the journey learn a great deal about their personal strengths and weaknesses and how they respond to challenge.

Those who summit the peak, as well as those who strive valiantly but fall short, are engaged in the critical factors of any success. These include careful preparation, the nimbleness to leverage knowledge to react in the moment, and the ability to balance self-reliance with knowing when to ask your team for help. Students also learn the value of recognizing when it is your time to step forward to lead and when it is your turn to follow. The lessons learned on the journey to the summit are not only essential to reach Kili's peak, but are also the basis for a lifetime of personal and professional success.

As you will read, the Elon University students who registered for the experiential course COR*331 Wilderness/Adventure Therapy and engaged with their faculty mentors embarked upon a journey of self-development that ultimately transformed their lives. They learned lessons that will make them better employees, friends, and human beings. As one student so eloquently stated, "Kilimanjaro was one of the most difficult things I have ever accomplished...by making it to the top I feel like I can accomplish anything in life." That is the power of experiential education, and the reason Elon University has invested so heavily in providing opportunities for students to learn by experiencing their education, embracing the challenge of going beyond what they believed was possible, and to soar.

These members of the Elon University community embody a zeal for learning and a fierce commitment to self-discovery. They exemplify why we have embraced engaged and experiential learning as the centerpiece of our model for student success. This commitment, supported by faculty members who are experts in delivering this mode of learning, has propelled Elon University into the national spotlight as consistently the number one university in the nation for study abroad and the number two institution for undergraduate teaching.

Along with their university faculty mentors, Elon sends a larger percentage of students to study away from campus each year than any other college or university in the United States. The Kilimanjaro course is a prime example of the university's Core Capstone seminars that align the developmental goals of global citizenship and intercultural competency. Faculty members develop these courses with embedded travel components to enrich the educational experience, using innovative teaching strategies to expand and deepen student learning opportunities.

This book captures the experiential learning experience of students and faculty who bonded—and learned—by facing a common hardship and embracing challenge in the pursuit of excellence and a new level of understanding. As you will read, each student, in their own way, succeeded. As one student wrote, "The depth of the relationships and friendships I made in this course will last a lifetime." The learning will, as well. I hope you find inspiration, as I have done, in the pages that follow.

Prologue

Dr. Rodney Parks

It's a complicated time to be a college professor. These days, students feel pressured to be perfect at everything they do, which can make it incredibly difficult for them to stretch themselves beyond their comfort zone and try new things. Students with this mindset can feel overwhelmed at the prospect of attempting something they may not immediately be good at, as they face both intrinsic and extrinsic pressure to perform in a way that upholds their own self-image and the image they want others to see. As a result, some students internalize failure, diminishing their self-confidence and negatively influencing their perception of themselves and their surroundings.

I always remind my students that after college they have limitless choices, even though students often feel they have very few. Many students in the Kilimanjaro course longed for adventure but felt boxed in by what they perceived as the inevitable "next step." In fact, it's common for students to feel a gnawing discontent when they settle into a major, a career, and a life.

Even, or perhaps especially, for those of us with a few more years under our belts, it's important to consider how each of us will ultimately measure our lives. Fear of failure and fear of the unknown are two of the emotions that most strongly motivate or discourage people who contemplate making changes or trying something new. Most people live for the rewards of success, especially the positive affirmation they receive from others who admire or seek to emulate that success. Students, like all of us, can become so preoccupied with achieving and maintaining a certain image of success that they are afraid to try anything new. Students in my classes often express the belief that there is no room for mistakes in a society that worships success and a culture imbued with perfectionism.

What does all this have to do with climbing a mountain? The students in this class unanimously agree that climbing Kilimanjaro was not easy. In fact, they characterized our last night on the trail as a "military-style death march to the top." Nearly eight hours of a constant vertical climb in the cold darkness of Kilimanjaro tests both physical stamina and mental strength. Each step is more difficult than the last, hands and feet are frozen, and the climbers experience a heightened sense of shared hardship in that moment. Students often talk about the support they provided one another on that last night, everyone pushing hard not to let the group down and doing their best to encourage one another. The students all say it's an experience they'll never forget.

Trekking a barren mountain face in arctic weather can get the best of you and your abilities. Yet the desire to make it to the top with the rest of the group and experience the sunrise on Mt. Kilimanjaro pushed us onward and upward. We shared an overwhelming collective commitment to never give up, to make it to the top, recognizing that "if I can do this, I can do anything." This is a lesson I hope my students will always remember when life gets really tough.

Pole pole ("Slowly, slowly" in Swahili) is encouraged on the journey, to give every climber the optimal chance of summiting. Reaching the top is something one earns, along with confidence in one's own mental resiliency and bragging rights for achieving one's dreams. Seeing that sunrise on Kilimanjaro after the endless night of hiking is an experience that is impossible to put into words. That fleeting moment with the students on Kilimanjaro was magical, the shared journey and camaraderie creating a feeling of oneness with nature and with each other. As one student noted in his final journal entry, "I would never want to go back and hike Kilimanjaro. I want to remember what it felt like at the top with the people I was with."

The feeling of summiting is addictive, the spirit of adventure pervasive, even as the course ends. As a group, we reflected on the challenge and our desire to continue conquering mountains. The classic wisdom reminding us not to look at the whole mountain, but instead to take it one piece at a time, is something each student comes to understand.

Let the adventure begin...

Why Teach through Experiential Education?

Dr. Carol A. Smith

If the disruption caused by COVID-19 has shown us anything, it's the value of adaptability in the face of upheaval. It's the power of agency and the ability to acknowledge and direct one's learning...workers who are adaptable and resilient will be the most sought-after.
Dr. David Schuler (2020, p. 1)

"Resilient learning," defined by Sterling (2010) as personal growth or competencies associated with healthy development and life success (e.g., social competence, sense of purpose, interest in learning), is a key objective for my classroom. Resilient students are socially competent, demonstrate a genuine interest in learning, and exude a sense of purpose. These statements pertaining to resiliency and adaptability resonate, as I want my students to be mentally nimble and agile.

Experiential education provides a transformative pedagogy that enhances resiliency and adaptability. According to the Association for Experiential Education (n.d.):

Experiential education is a teaching philosophy that informs many methodologies in which educators purposefully engage with learners in direct experience and focused reflections in order to increase knowledge, develop skills, clarify values, and develop people's capacity to contribute to their communities.

The teaching philosophy of John Dewey, considered by some to be "the most significant educational thinker of his era" (Levin, n.d.), parallels the methodology of experiential education. Dewey's progressive education asserted that students must be invested in what they learn, rather than simply performing rote memorization, and that the curriculum should be relevant to students' lives. He saw education becoming disconnected from students' development as human beings and members of society due to the increased industrialization of education.

Dewey saw learning by doing and the development of practical life skills as crucial to education. Unlike many of his contemporaries, he proposed a greater connection between education and society, arguing that education should prepare children to become productive contributors to humanity (Dewey, 1972). Rather than viewing education as disconnected from the "real world," Dewey believed that school must "avoid the teaching of abstract ideas; rather, it must provide actual conditions out of which ideas grow" (Spring, 2018, p. 285).

Teaching is my true passion, particularly teaching students in the outdoors and investing in their holistic well-being. Striving to be an exemplary teacher is not only part of my work but is central to who I am as a teacher. I believe in the importance of challenging my students to be engaged learners.

Dewey also advocated for a different approach to teaching, suggesting that teachers should act as facilitators who guide engagement and present opportunities for students to choose from. Even in his early writing, Dewey advocated for a hands-on approach to education that allowed for experimentation, application, and engagement. It is impossible for teachers to be successful if students don't listen and participate. This is how we extend learning beyond the classroom and develop transferable skills that help students to succeed post-university.

I want my students not just to regurgitate information, but to learn—I want them to use their skills to extrapolate what they learn to the real world post-graduation. In Dewey's view, "education which does not occur through forms of life, forms that are worth living for their own sake, is always a poor substitute for the genuine reality and tends to cramp and to deaden" children's natural impulses and excitement (Dewey, 1972, p. 87). Effective teaching promotes the intellectual vitality of the university and the wider community. While its primary focus is the transmission of knowledge and the development of new skills and insights, teaching is not limited to the classroom setting.

Dewey's approach represented a significant departure from how teachers and teaching were viewed previously. He advocated for "learning by doing, relating material to the interests of the child, and doing projects" rather than the traditional rote memorization (Spring, 2018, p. 287). Dewey's work, and by extension my pedagogical style of purpose outside the classroom, highlights a critical emphasis of experiential education.

Some critics argued that under Dewey's system students would fail to acquire basic academic skills and knowledge, as his methodology was seen as a no-rules approach that allowed children to "do whatever they want." Experiential education is the active process of learning through experience, with the further parameter of learning through the practice of reflection rather than memorization (Beard, 2018). Beard (2018, p. 27) writes that Dewey considered "experience as an optimal stimulus for learning." Rather than conducting class as a "sage on the stage," teachers act as facilitators who guide the experience of their students. This calls for a change in the relationship between teacher and student (Adams et al., 1997; Association for Experiential Learning, n.d.; Kumashiro, 2015).

The criticism of experiential education that continues today is very similar to the criticism Dewey faced. Although they might look like educational spaces with no rules, in which students do whatever they want, experiential education settings are in fact highly facilitated, structured, and sequenced learning environments. In progressive education settings, students are given choices about their learning and the ways in which they want to be challenged.

Whereas some might see chaos in this approach, I see "controlled chaos" in the student-centered classroom. This choice does *not* mean teachers are not guiding the process; in fact, the opposite is true. As facilitators, teachers provide students with a series of intentional, carefully designed opportunities that lead to meaningful learning experiences.

This empowerment to decide heightens the quality of the classroom experience. "Students learn that this freedom [to choose] is directly connected to their disposition for being responsible as an individual and member of society" (Goodman & Kuzmic, 1997, p. 84). My classroom does look different from more traditional classrooms; fortunately, I have supportive administrators who recognize its benefits. Fostering experiential education as a philosophical or conceptual preference provides opportunities to advance and further my sphere of influence in the educational realm.

A statement from a student evaluation for one of my classes highlights the value of Dewey's approach. The student noted the value of the experiential education course in

> balancing between letting us take the lead/learn through trial and error and prompting us to reflect on various aspects to ensure that we are making the connections we need to learn the most from the activities. It's an incredibly authentic and relevant class…a class that we all respect, take seriously, and value for everything it teaches us.

Students engaged in experiential education are engrossed in the practice of critical reflection through discussion, engaged learning activities, and writing assignments. Although the readings and expectations vary according to course focus, level, and scaffolding needed, the underlying skills emphasized remain constant. Classes are discussion-based, a pedagogical approach that includes a mixture of individual, small group, and large group learning activities aligned with the learning objectives for the day and course.

Such variety provides opportunities for both extroverted and introverted students to learn and share ideas. Students then feel they have something to contribute that is valuable and valued. They praise the opportunity to engage in many forms of learning, "from discussions on readings to . . . reflections" and the ability to participate in a "truly respectful and collaborative class environment."

Students enrolled in experiential education classes implicitly understand and support Dewey's philosophy. One student who participated in the multi-vine element of a ropes course noted, "My biggest takeaway from this activity is this: you cannot walk the wire alone. Life will throw hurdles your way, and though you may stumble and fall, you have to allow the people around you to help you get across."

Also referring to the multi-vine, another student wrote:

I...wasn't going to get on again after my second failed attempt...I felt so proud of myself and my heart was beating a mile a minute once I got down. I want to carry that feeling of accomplishment, and courage to try again throughout my life...I was able to not be afraid to give up and find it within myself to keep trying even after I've failed. Personal growth was not something I thought I would gain from this class, but I've been surprised and pleased with myself for how much personal growth I've managed to do in such a short time period.

The methodology of direct experiences and focused reflections espoused by the Association for Experiential Education (AEE), which reflects Dewey's approach, is the epitome of what I do in my classroom. As facilitator-teachers, our role is to assist students in uncovering solutions by developing skills such as critical thinking and problem solving. Demonstrating the value of lifelong learning is crucial, as is encouraging students to be curious and passionate about what they do. Students discover how to learn, innovate, collaborate, and communicate their ideas to others. We are facilitators of knowledge, leveling the playing field for students, decentralizing the power in the classroom, and affirming the value of students' existing knowledge and the background they bring to the classroom. Our mission is to help students *learn how* to learn and *learn how* to think; it is not to teach students *what to think* about whatever the topic might be. This process may require failing before they can succeed. And that is okay. Dewey would be proud.

Additionally, it is critical to link learning together. We don't live in silos, and neither should we teach in silos. Most knowledge can be related to other fields of study and we must connect subjects. Facilitator-teachers approach each class with a goal of fostering long-term, authentic learning. To achieve this aim, we must develop and apply methods to make the curriculum rigorous and relevant. It is also important that faculty take the material and extrapolate it beyond the classroom, making it relevant so that students want to learn.

Students must feel safe enough to fully invest in the class. I strive to make my classroom a safe place; often we think only about physical safety, but emotional safety is equally crucial for learning to take place. I encourage all students to achieve the potential I see in them, which they may not yet see in themselves. A few words of encouragement can go a long way in helping them reach this full potential.

As a facilitator of knowledge, I believe in the importance of decentralizing power by including students in the learning process, giving them choices about what to learn and how to proceed. Students bring to the classroom their own knowledge, background, and history. When they feel a sense of ownership in the classroom environment, they are more invested in the outcome. Experiential education puts teachers and students on a more equal level as it recognizes that both groups have valuable knowledge and viewpoints, rather than promoting the belief that the teacher has all the information. "Questioning differences that arise from these multiple perspectives is the fuel for learning and new insights. Challenging the expert's viewpoint even becomes possible" (Kolb & Kolb, 2017, p. xxv). This ability to challenge existing views on control within the classroom is an important part of experiential education. De-centering knowledge and changing the teacher's role to that of a facilitator are key components of experiential education. Moreover, during the learning process the roles of educator and learner can be loosely defined and may shift (AEE, n.d.).

This approach keeps me on my toes in seeking to meet my students' learning needs. These methodologies force me to relinquish some control in the class, but with the benefit of seeing students improve their communication skills as they work in small groups, develop leadership skills as they seek to reach a consensus with their classmates, and learn the importance of cooperation. I love my "controlled chaos" in the student-centered classroom, as everyone is more involved. This makes my heart happy.

Outdoor adventure programs emphasize teamwork, problem solving, and collaboration in the context of being active and outdoors. These programs offer a variety of distinct activities that are grounded in the principle that "behavior impacts the outcome." When students do not accomplish the agreed-upon goal, they fail. They see the failure. They experience the failure. Participants are pushed beyond their comfort zone and learn what they are capable of accomplishing. When faced with an activity with high perceived risk yet low real risk, students can overcome fears, inhibitions, and self-doubt. After achieving the goal or overcoming some other (seemingly) insurmountable challenge, they realize they are capable of more sophisticated, more disciplined, and more challenging engagement than they previously believed.

Beneficial effects of participating in outdoor adventure programs include improvements in physical fitness, interpersonal and family functioning, group performance, social skills, self-esteem, internal locus of control, self-efficacy, and psychological symptoms such as depression and anxiety (Cason & Gillis, 1994; Gillis & Speelman, 2008; Hattie et al., 1997; Wilson & Lipsey, 2000). Meta-analyses indicate that the effects of outdoor adventure programs on these outcome criteria are reliable, with small to medium effect sizes (Hans, 2000).

Facilitation of outdoor adventure programs encompasses creating suitable experiences, posing problems, setting boundaries, supporting students, ensuring physical and emotional safety, and facilitating the learning process. Weekly writing supports the AEE Principle of Practice stating that experiential learning occurs when carefully chosen experiences are supported by reflection, critical analysis, and synthesis of the "what," "so what," and "now what" of our encounters. I do not rely on traditional testing methods; instead, in my classes, students are expected to reflect on our activities and write papers using these three questions to reflect on our experiences. These prompts are carefully chosen to encourage students to take initiative, make decisions about their activities, and be accountable for what happens. Throughout the semester, the self-reflective papers, journaling, class debriefs, and reflective writings on their experiences show an appreciation of the deliberateness of the experience. Research has shown that the more deliberate and authentic the task (in contrast to a contrived, in-class experience), the better the educational opportunity.

Activities need to be sequences that build on previous knowledge. Students must be actively engaged in posing questions, investigating, being curious, solving problems, and assuming responsibility, as the semester progresses from (physically, mentally, and emotionally) low-risk trust-building activities to higher-stakes challenges. When we are on the experiential campus and a challenge is presented, if students all stand around looking at each other nothing will be accomplished. I have been known to stand there upwards of five minutes while they mill around or freeze, waiting for me to tell them what to do. At some point, they realize they are driving this lesson — they will learn through active participation, not by passively receiving knowledge I spoon-feed them. Of course, I constantly monitor the threshold of frustration and step in with directed questions when needed, using guided discovery to gently direct them to a more productive path.

Relationships are developed and nurtured in this context. In most experiential education settings, mutual respect and relationships are critical to fostering authentic learning. My best evidence of this is the number of times students note in their reflections that they know their classmates, care about them, and become friends with them. One student reported:

> we all became pretty good friends. I never imagined that I would be close enough with an entire class that we would still talk in our group chat after the class had ended...I didn't know how to talk to someone that I didn't know, alone... We ended up mostly talking about football, which I know nothing about, but [a fellow student] also told me I should go to the games, and by the end of this semester I had been to four football games.

This perspective strongly aligns with Garrison's (2007) statement about the importance of social presence. Garrison developed what he calls the Five Design Principles of Resilient Teaching, the fourth of which resonates with me in relation to experiential education: relationship-rich engaged learning, consisting of the "social presence," "teacher presence," and "cognitive presence."

With social presence, students get to know and support one another. Teacher presence occurs when the students feel the teacher knows them and cares about them and their learning. Cognitive presence takes place when the students all think about, explore, and learn the course content (Garrison, 2007).

Because the outcomes of experience cannot reliably be predicted, students in experientially based classes learn from natural consequences, experiencing success, failure, adventure, risk-taking, and uncertainty. These outcomes of experiential education extend learning beyond the classroom. Many of our students do not view failure as an option, and as a result they struggle. Students are much more engaged when a class is more closely aligned with their wants. When students carefully choose an experience that is meaningful to them, they are more likely to be successful, and at the same time failure has more impact. Their reflection, critical analysis, and synthesis are more authentic when the results of the learning are personal and form the basis for future experience and learning.

I believe in the power of outdoor experiential education. I have seen my students grow in their self-confidence and belief in themselves. Their written comments and the manner in which they carry themselves in (and outside of) class change. They believe they can be successful. They are "resilient learners" in Sterling's (2010) definition, experiencing personal growth in the competencies associated with healthy development and life success (e.g., social competence, sense of purpose, interest in learning); demonstrating a genuine interest in learning; and exuding a sense of purpose (Duckworth et al., 2007; Sterling, 2010).

A final reflection from one of my students conveys the genuine value and impact of experiential education:

Over the last nine months, I have been given challenges, but I've also watched myself (with help) overcome those challenges, which is the true beauty of adventure-based learning. I've been reflecting a lot lately on the major. At first, I wasn't sure why I liked it. Other classes tend to come more easily to me, partially because I'm really good at processing things intellectually but struggle more to process things emotionally. Then I realized that was why I liked it—because it's hard, because it's challenging, because it forces me to use my strengths and develop my areas for growth, because it shows me that I can do hard things and succeed, because it forces me to acknowledge that I am capable.

About the Author

Dr. Carol A. Smith, Professor of Education & Wellness, School of Education, Elon University, Elon, NC, USA

I was destined to teach. I come from a family of teachers: My mom taught kindergarten, my sister taught elementary physical education, and my brother-in-law taught kinesiology at the university level. My brother majored in physical education but taught woodworking in high school. My sister-in-law, a school librarian, was the outlier. My husband has degrees in physical education but is a woodworker who teaches woodworking. My dad was also a woodworker.

I was teaching at a university in a non-tenure track role but lost my summer position due to funding cuts. Pragmatically, I wanted job security, so I decided to pursue a terminal degree. My educational preparation is eclectic: I have degrees in physical education and teacher education (BS from University of Massachussets/Amherst and MEd from Frostburg State College in Maryland); my PhD is in Kinesiology (Texas A&M University/ College Station) with a concentration in outdoor education/ adventure-based learning. I have been at Elon University since 1999 and currently serve as the Program Coordinator of the Adventure-Based Learning curriculum.

Chapter 1

Introduction

Victoria Baumgarten and Dara Sypes

In January 2020, Elon University, a small, private liberal arts university in North Carolina, introduced an innovative study abroad course that applied the practices of wilderness and adventure therapy to an opportunity to hike Mt. Kilimanjaro in Tanzania, East Africa. This four-week class was offered primarily to juniors and seniors who were interested in applying for the pilot program. In March 2019, approximately 60 students applied to participate in the program. Dr. Rodney Parks, the university's registrar, had been working to create the program over the previous several years. Because this class was such a large undertaking, professors Kelly Reimer, the Director of Teaching and Learning Technologies, and Kristen Aquilino, the Director of International Student Services, joined the class, and each contributed significantly to the overall well-being of the students and the success of the course.

Dr. Parks had led an adventure therapy class on the Inca Trail in Peru annually during Thanksgiving break. After offering that course for 10 years, he began to push himself further to ask, "Where else in the world can students learn about wilderness therapy and embark on a new summiting experience?" From this question the original idea to peak Kilimanjaro was born.

This book, written collaboratively by 22 student authors, represents the culmination of our class's experience on the trail. In these chapters each student strives to articulate what Kilimanjaro meant to them. Despite each author's individual experiences, we all agree that the following quote from writer

René Daumal in his book *Mt. Analogue* feels very applicable to our journey:

> You cannot stay on the summit forever; you have to come down again. So why bother in the first place? Just this: What is above knows what is below, but what is below does not know what is above. One climbs, one sees. One descends, one sees no longer, but one has seen. There is an art of conducting oneself in the lower regions by the memory of what one saw higher up. When one can no longer see, one can at least still know.

We hope this book provides a way for our class to remember what we saw at the summit. We also hope it helps readers who have not had the same opportunities, resources, or privileges we have had to see what we saw from above and bring it back down with them below. Additionally, our class wants to provide future hikers with a resource we didn't feel was available to us. We want to help guide people on their journey and pass along any information that might be helpful, so young adults can continue to make more memories on that mountain.

Due to the application deadlines for our university's study abroad program, the class committed to Kilimanjaro almost a year in advance of the trip. In April 2019, shortly after being accepted into the program, the class had its first meeting. In this meeting, students were asked to describe why they had signed up for the trip, which sparked personal reflection and deeper thinking as to why this group, which represented diverse majors, ages, and interests, was coming together to take on Kilimanjaro.

Although every student had their own unique motivation for signing up, their reasons also clearly had some continuity. Victoria, a senior business student, wanted to make a change and expand her horizons. Having returned from a study abroad experience in New Zealand just months before, she still had a strong desire to travel and craved the excitement of trying new things.

After only a few months back in North Carolina, Victoria found herself bored with the typical semester routine, feeling that college was the time to be adventurous. As a business major planning to start a corporate job following graduation, she was getting antsy, reminding herself that this could be the last getaway she would be fortunate enough to take for a while. She also recognized that in a year she would be grateful for the opportunity to get off campus again, acknowledging that she had always struggled with an inability to sit still and settle into a routine.

For these reasons, Victoria started looking at options for Winter Term study abroad classes offered in January. She looked at the costs and her remaining graduation requirements and was drawn to a few potential trips. When she came across the Kilimanjaro class, she began to consider whether this was the trip for her.

At first, she looked at the trip out of curiosity, but then she started to think about how summiting Kilimanjaro would be the ideal way to end her college adventure. Victoria acknowledges that she was driven by the desire to be able to say she had climbed Mt. Kilimanjaro, a motivation many students admitted was part of their decision process. But Victoria had also done a lot of hiking in New Zealand and wanted to take this hobby to the next level.

For the next few months, she began to prepare for the trip physically, but mentally she had not yet processed what she had signed up for. She viewed Kilimanjaro as a physical challenge and an end goal, as opposed to a step in her personal growth. Yet as the trip approached, she realized that the mental battle of summiting Kilimanjaro would be just as important as the physical challenge, and her excitement and nervousness about what lay ahead truly began to develop.

Dara described herself as being a completely different person when she signed up for the course a year earlier. Dara had never been abroad during her time at Elon and was lucky enough to have the opportunity to go abroad for her final Winter Term. When she first started looking at the list of programs, none of them called out to her until she saw "Wilderness and Adventure Therapy on Mt. Kilimanjaro." As a senior public health and psychology double major, the course title immediately grabbed her attention. On a more personal level, her mental health at the time was poor and she was candidly ready for a life-changing journey.

Dara's childhood best friend had recently completed a three-month wilderness therapy program in Costa Rica and came home a changed person with a new outlook on life. Seeing such a drastic shift in her friend left Dara curious as to what wilderness therapy was all about; she was ready to learn more. In the months leading up to the trip, she embarked on a journey of personal growth in which she began to take her mental health more seriously. She did this primarily by completing a 200-hour yoga teacher-training course.

During this time, Dara learned more about how her brain worked and reflected on what she hoped to gain from this experience. Her biggest personal goal for Kilimanjaro at this point was to get more comfortable being uncomfortable. In retrospect, Dara cannot believe how quickly she achieved that goal.

As the trip grew closer, many students realized that their expectations from a year earlier had shifted and evolved. This became particularly evident once the group was on the trail and the talk turned to reflections on why each member of the class had chosen to be part of this experimental trip. Nevertheless, although Victoria, Dara, and their classmates signed up for different reasons and learned different lessons from the trip, everyone experienced the journey together.

Preparations

Our class took the Machame route, a six-day trek. There are several different climbing options that range from six to 10 days. The shorter the hike up, the lower the summit success rate becomes, because less acclimation time increases the likelihood of altitude sickness. But since every extra day spent on the mountain increases the cost of the trip, the professors chose the six-day option to keep the course as affordable as possible.

Notably, one of the demographic groups that is most likely *not* to make it to the summit is 18- to 30-year-old men, because they are typically overconfident and do not go at the recommended *"pole pole"* ("slowly, slowly") pace. Even though the odds felt a little stacked against us, we remained cautiously optimistic that we would be able to say not only that we had hiked Mt. Kilimanjaro, but also that we hiked it in the shortest amount of time for a tourist group.

One of the many ways in which this experience is unique is that there is a lengthy packing list of items the average person may not already own. It is important to keep in mind that this is a short trip, so gear can be borrowed or rented to keep costs down. The class learned that the items on the packing list are there for a reason and help make the trip manageable. But there are always exceptions to the rule. Our classmate Jack summited the mountain in Skechers, but even he said he would not recommend this.

No two packing lists will look exactly the same, and we learned the importance of choosing which things to splurge on and which to save on. For example, some students splurged on a Gore-Tex rain jacket and rain pants while buying trekking poles from Walmart. There is no need to have brand-name gear for everything, especially when cost is a real concern. However, it's also important to keep in mind that what might feel unnecessary at home could turn into a critical item on the trail. After completing the trek, this is the packing list we recommend.

Clothing

- Rain jacket
- Down jacket (must be warm for the summit)
- Two long-sleeve, moisture-wicking shirts
- Two short-sleeve, moisture-wicking shirts
- Rain pants
- Two pairs of hiking pants
- Fleece pants
- Long underwear
- Wool shirt
- Fleece shirt or jacket
- Clean pair of clothes used for camp/sleeping

Headwear

- Brimmed hat
- Knit hat
- Balaclava
- Buff or bandana

Handwear

- Thin pair of gloves (waterproof)
- Ski gloves (waterproof)

Footwear

- Waterproof hiking boots
- Shoes to wear at campsite
- Wool socks (3–5 pairs, but more if you are opting to go on the longer route)
- Sock liners/thin socks for blisters (optional)

Accessories

- Sunglasses
- Waterproof backpack cover
- Water bladder (3 liters)

- Nalgene water bottle
- Quick-dry towel
- Stuff sacks/dry bags

Equipment

- Daypack (this should be light, around 35 liters)
- Duffel bag (around 50–90 liters)
- Zero-degree Fahrenheit sleeping bag (depending on the company, can be rented)
- Trekking poles (depending on the company, can be rented)
- Camp pillow
- Headlamp
- Batteries for headlamp
- Sleeping-bag liner (if you sleep cold)
- Portable charger/solar charger
- Power converter for hotel
- Medications
- Sunscreen
- Bug spray
- Hand sanitizer
- Wilderness wipes
- Snacks (bring more than you think you'll need)
- Ziploc bags (a duct-taped bag for toilet waste)
- Toilet paper
- Electrolytes
- Lip balm/Vaseline
- Contacts and glasses
- Toiletries
- Passport
- Visa

For Women

- 1–2 pairs of leggings (good for layering)

- Tampons/pads/liners
- Dry shampoo or baby powder

The class quickly learned to value routine while on the mountain. Whether it was taking time to put on fresh socks before bed, wiping yourself down with baby wipes, or reading a book in your tent, routine will feel precious after a long day of hiking. This is also not the time to cut out caffeine or experiment with a new diet. We all learned from experience that the altitude can mess with your body, so be prepared for things to go wrong. For example, some of our classmates regularly wear contacts, but due to the change in climate, they had to switch to glasses. Women may experience menstruation due to the altitude. Unexpected things will happen. Be prepared.

Vaccinations and Medications

Before the trip, all Kilimanjaro hikers are advised to see their doctor or visit a travel clinic. It is important to do research on the CDC (Centers for Disease Control) website to see which vaccinations are recommended and ask specifically for those you think you will need. For our trip, we were advised to have typhoid, tetanus, MMR, measles, and Hepatitis A vaccinations. In addition, you will also need a prescription for malaria medication as well as Diamox. While Diamox is not required, it is extremely useful to help with altitude adjustment. The side effects of Diamox include tingling in the extremities, a lack of appetite, and constant urination, so weigh the pros and cons accordingly. Kenny, a Denver native, decided to take prescription headache medication instead of Diamox and he was still able to summit. So not taking Diamox is an option, but a somewhat riskier one.

We also strongly recommend a form of Imodium or an antibiotic for traveler's diarrhea. Almost everyone's stomach got weird at some point and with new foods also being introduced, it felt like a recipe for disaster. A vast majority of our class had these issues and everyone was thankful to have over-the-counter medication to help. We also recommend general medications like Advil, Pepto-Bismol, and Dramamine because, as a general rule, it's important to be prepared.

Physical Preparation

This is a trip that requires a great deal of physical preparation and it is really not the time to be out of shape. Our class learned quickly that in order to succeed, we were going to have to hit the gym. For six months before our departure, we would see each other at our campus gym walking on the StairMaster or jogging around campus. This community accountability and encouragement was something we all found helpful. Even though most people do not summit Kilimanjaro with 21 other young adults, find a community of people to get in shape with. Katherine and Abby, two roommates in the class, found a lot of motivation in going to the gym together, and the physical preparation made the peak even more special.

That being said, there is no specific workout plan you need to follow. Cardio fitness will be key to increasing your endurance for the long climb ahead. This is essentially a very long walk and your muscles will need to be prepared for the extended repetitive movements. Exercises like day hikes, long walks, stationary biking, and the StairMaster will be useful. Every day on the hike we carried our daypacks, so when we worked out it was important for us to think about engaging our core, back, and shoulder strength.

We also found that squats were very important. One suggestion a few members of the class enjoyed was to listen to the song "Halo" by Beyoncé and do a squat every time she sings the word "halo." We were sore and laughing by the end of the song and our legs were just a little more prepared for Summit Night. Other members of the class suggested planning a camping trip with friends before traveling to Tanzania. Any amount of physical preparation will help, even if it is just practicing getting a full night's sleep in a sleeping bag. Also keep in mind that no matter how prepared you are, the hike will be difficult for everyone—but it is also unquestionably worth it. Regardless of how you choose to prepare physically, attitude and mental preparation will be the most important factors for a successful climb.

Mental Preparation

Our class found that the most challenging element of hiking Kilimanjaro was the mental battle that took place inside us all. We also quickly learned that our bodies were capable of much more than we had initially expected. If future Kilimanjaro hikers can manage to maintain a positive attitude through the hardships of the climb and do not experience any forms of altitude sickness that are beyond their control, their bodies will get them to the top. We learned the importance of listening to your body and acknowledging that there are certain kinds of altitude sickness you cannot control. It takes mental strength to determine when to stop pushing your body forward.

It is vital to assess your mental health before getting on the mountain. Our class did this by setting personal goals that identified how we wanted to grow during this experience. Dara, the yogi, and other members of the class learned that it was critical to acknowledge and accept where they were mentally before the trip, because mental and physical barriers will arise unexpectedly on Kilimanjaro. Being honest with ourselves and our classmates, we learned, was essential.

In addition, the local guides didn't just guide us physically; they also provided psychological support and motivation. Even though the hike looked almost easy for them, they had compassion for us and expressed how proud they were of us after we completed each day's hike. Sharing with our guides any feelings we were experiencing was a helpful tool that many of us utilized. Remember that guides are meant to be a resource for hikers when they are struggling. They're there for a reason.

During Summit Night, we all admitted that we could focus only on taking the next step. We felt we would get distracted by looking up and focusing on how much more distance we had to go. Each step felt somewhat manageable, but the entire hike seemed almost overwhelmingly daunting. Looking too far ahead would cause unnecessary worry about elements we were unable to control.

In a way, our climb served as a metaphor for life outside of hiking. Anxiety and stress can come from looking too far ahead and not focusing on the daily, manageable tasks. Being aware of every step we took kept us present and reduced the feeling of being overwhelmed. Both peers and guides were incredibly important, because keeping conversation going or singing a song while focusing on the small steps helped us mentally and made the entire experience more enjoyable. Putting this step-by-step mental tool into practice felt like a lesson we could take off the mountain and into our everyday lives.

Throughout this book, we will describe the ups and downs of our journey together as a class. The struggles and triumphs we experienced created deep bonds between all 25 of us. Even the most difficult challenges comprised an extremely important part of our story as a group, and, though it may sound cheesy to say, we would not have changed a thing. Although some of the stories may be intimidating, this was truly an experience that allowed us to gain newfound confidence and perspective that we can take from above and apply to our lives below.

Chapter 2

The Town of Moshi

Neel Dhanani and Cole Kocjancic

Our class began the journey to Tanzania with an hour-long bus ride to the airport followed by a short plane ride to Washington, DC, a 13-hour flight to Ethiopia, and lastly a quick two-hour flight to the Kilimanjaro airport. By the time we touched down in this long-anticipated country we were exhausted and unsure of the correct time of day. Our class quickly grouped together and went through Customs with relative ease.

Our duffel bags and backpacks created an almost embarrassingly huge pile in the baggage claim area; it looked like our class was sponsored by Patagonia. After every bag was accounted for, some class members exchanged US dollars for Tanzanian shillings. However, most of the more touristy places we flocked to happily accepted US dollars. So we recommend exchanging $60 or less, and if you have some extra at the end of your trip, the shillings make an excellent souvenir as well.

When we exited the airport, our bus driver greeted us with a friendly "*JAMBOOO*," which means "hello" and is typically used for tourists. While we found our seats, the guides whom we would soon meet tossed our bags on top of the bus. It looked like a Tanzanian version of *The Beverly Hillbillies*. After everyone was settled, we headed to the town of Moshi.

We had no idea what to expect once the bus left the airport gates and continued down the bumpy road toward the hotel. Having no expectations was quite all right because it allowed us to have an open and clear mindset, which is crucial when entering unfamiliar territory. That said, there is a clear distinction between letting go of expectations and ignorantly entering a different culture. We had learned through class discussions the importance of ethical tourism, which in this country can be quite tricky, especially when so many people are willing to cater to Americans. Letting go of expectations is a great way to be open-minded when embarking on a trip, but we also knew it was important to do our research beforehand to learn about the culture and context we were entering.

As we drove toward Moshi, it quickly became apparent that the rules of the road in Tanzania were quite different from what we were used to in the US. Witnessing traffic from the opposite side of the road was unsettling at first, but with time we began to get used to it. The majority of vehicles on the road tend to be motorcycles, buses, semi-trucks, and smaller vehicles instead of the family cars we typically see in the US. Motorcyclists dominate the road, passing on either the right or left side whenever they choose. Instead of taking the naps our bodies craved, our eyes were glued to the bus windows.

Another unusual aspect of driving we witnessed while heading toward Moshi was that there were no traffic lights. We learned that some roundabouts could get pretty chaotic when there were three or four motorcycles within arm's length of our vehicle. Fortunately there are plenty of stop signs and crosswalks that control the flow of traffic. However, the scenery from the airport to Moshi is much more captivating than Tanzania's traffic laws.

At the beginning of the journey to our hotel, the road seemed to carelessly carve a path through sunflower-filled fields. It is quite a spectacular sight to see streets lined with trees and sunflowers against the contrast of the deep blue sky. As the trip progressed, however, the sunflower fields steadily transformed into endless fields of grasses, crops, and animal pastures.

Often in Tanzania, extended families and entire villages work together to maintain a shared agricultural field. The primary crops grown in the Moshi region include maize and beans, both crops that thrive in the extensive rainy season. Other crops grown just outside Moshi include coffee beans, plantains, and bananas in the high-altitude, nutrient-rich soil, while just south of Moshi are vast fields of sugarcane. Agriculture accounts for a large portion of Moshi's economic sustainability, so producing a successful harvest is vital to the economic success of the region. Glimpsing the vastness of the agricultural fields made us all appreciate the hard work and dedication it takes to have a successful harvest year.

In addition to plant-based agriculture, animal agriculture is a fundamental necessity for Tanzanian culture. The animals we saw in the villages along the countryside included goats, chickens, and cows. In addition, other animals, such as mules, assist with the harvesting process as opposed to being served on the dinner table.

As the bus continued on its route to the hotel, Neel, the most relaxed member of our group, observed the variety of methods for raising livestock. He noted that some chickens were caged while others roamed free, plucking at the grass for an easy meal. The cows and goats seemed to have even more freedom as they roamed through the fields and along the roadside in groups guided by younger children, with occasional assistance from a herding dog. Even from a distance we could see the enormous effort and responsibility required to raise and provide for these animals.

After being on the bus for some time, a few of us started to develop an appetite, likely from turning down the Ethiopian Airlines food on the plane. Our hunger could also have been due to the street vendors attempting to sell cooked corn on the cob to every passerby. Most of the meals served at the hotel where we stayed included a protein source, a vegetable side, and some rice. Before almost every meal, we were served a warm bowl of soup, typically composed of savory bananas and other vegetables. Cole, a junior engineering student, advises any Tanzanian traveler to get used to the soup because it will be served at just about every meal. We all acquired a strong affinity for some types of the soup and questioned why Chunky or Campbell's had not yet added these flavors to their inventory. However, the pre-meal soup did get old much more quickly than we anticipated, especially on our journey up and down Mt. Kilimanjaro. Although this information may sound trivial, any traveler will quickly understand what we mean.

We found that the most common protein dishes were comprised of either chicken or beef. Notably, the protein we were served was not full of additives or chemicals such as antibiotics, which we are accustomed to in the US. Instead, the chickens and cows were raised on natural diets and in favorable environments. Maybe it was just our excitement to try these new foods, but we all agreed that the meat tasted better in Tanzania than in the Elon dining halls. As for the vegetable side, we ate corn, beans, plantains, asparagus, and even green beans. Although none of the types of vegetables were totally foreign, they were all cooked differently and seasoned in a way that was unfamiliar. It took a few meals for us all to figure out what our taste buds preferred, but we were all committed to remaining open to new types of dishes. We wanted to learn about Tanzanian culture and experience the country to the fullest extent, and food was one key way to do that.

As we rode from the airport to the hotel, some of our class members started drifting off to sleep, while those still awake noticed construction on the side of the road or watched the changes in scenery. One second the bus was surrounded by what felt like endless fields, while the next moment we found ourselves driving through a town. Our groggy heads perked up to pay attention to the activity occurring outside. We saw people lounging in the shade and next to some motorcycles. Other locals were working hard at an automotive repair store. Occasionally we caught the eye of someone observing the bus full of tourists as it passed by.

However, we all agreed that the highlight of traveling through these villages and towns was seeing all the children rush to the bus, waving with endless enthusiasm and excitement. Most of the children wore matching uniforms, having just finished school for the day. We had the opportunity to learn about the education system in Tanzania through a conversation with our bus driver. We learned that most children attend school at a very early age for a couple of years, where they learn basic subjects such as math, reading, and the Swahili language. This stage in education is referred to as pre-primary education and is followed by primary education.

In primary school, as students proceed through the grade levels, math, reading, history, and language become more specialized, and English is taught as a second language. Some classes are even taught in English to accelerate the learning of the language. After graduating from primary school, some students advance to secondary school, where technical skills and subjects become very specialized. This felt very different from our liberal arts education at Elon, which allows for a wide breadth of knowledge in many disciplines.

Moving on from secondary school depends heavily on grades and overall success in the classroom. The government provides testing for students who have exhibited success or have the potential to achieve success through more schooling. Students who score high on the exam are eligible to receive further education. Education at this subsequent level is synonymous with a college education, where students focus on specialized subjects that direct them to their profession.

Only a handful of the students who graduate from primary school have the opportunity to proceed through higher levels of education. Typically, a pre-primary school can be found in every village to provide every child with easy access to basic education. Secondary schools, on the other hand, are much more geographically dispersed due to the limited number of students who are given the opportunity to attend secondary school.

One notable difference between American and Tanzanian students is that Tanzanian students tend to love school and have a positive outlook on education. In contrast, many students in the US seem to resent school and hold negative attitudes toward it. This depressing reality may be challenging to overcome. We engaged in many conversations about education with the bus drivers, porters, and guides. The locals we met were very curious about the American education system and we were excited to learn anything we could about the local culture.

As the children smiled and waved at us, it was impossible not to smile back. Some of the children were holding books while others were carrying small backpacks. Behind the waving students, we noticed friendly soccer competitions taking place in the background. In Tanzania, only a couple of sports are recognized, and none are honored as much as soccer. By far the most popular sport in the country, soccer is played at nearly every level. Some schools have a soccer team that competes against soccer teams from nearby schools in friendly yet highly competitive matches. If you pay close attention, some of the locals may be listening to a soccer match on the radio or perhaps watching a match on the television in a bar or restaurant. There have also been several legendary runners, in both short and long distances, who came from Tanzania. As we sat patiently on the bus gazing out the windows, we hoped to see some runners on the side of the road.

When the bus was only a few miles from the hotel, we noticed that the traffic seemed to pick up and alongside the roads the scenery became more crowded. The number of stores, vendors, houses, and people lining the sides of the street increased noticeably. This is a sure sign that you have entered the town of Moshi.

Most of the businesses lining the streets are privately owned by individuals who provide the public with essential goods and services. You may be able to identify specific businesses such as a paint store, a lumber provider, and restaurants. Many of the restaurants have an outdoor dining area where people can enjoy a nice meal in the shade, protected from the sun. However, when it is raining the streets and roadsides become much less populated. Moshi is known for its variable climate, where a bright and sunny day in one moment can give way to a torrential downpour in the next. Varying weather patterns are the norm for this region and they only become more unpredictable while climbing Mt. Kilimanjaro.

After traveling on the same road for about an hour, the bus suddenly turned down a side road. As it continued down the bumpy side road, we couldn't help but wonder, "Where are they taking us?" Neel noticed the small liquor and convenience stores lining the side road, and as the bus progressed on its journey, we finally saw the hotel gate, before spotting the hotel itself.

When the gate opened the gatekeeper gave us a friendly wave, easing our nerves and increasing our excitement. The bus finally came to a stop and everyone eagerly got out to stretch and breathe some fresh air. We had successfully made it through Moshi to the hotel and had acquired a fresh perspective on the town, the people, and the culture. We grabbed our backpacks and duffel bags, headed to the hotel, and finally grabbed that Kilimanjaro beer we had all been waiting for.

Chapter 3

The History, Climate, and Ecosystems of Mt. Kilimanjaro

Emma Renfro and Daniela Nasser

Image from Secret Compass:
The Geography, People, and Mythology of
Africa's Highest Peak.
Courtesy of the Tanzania Wilderness and Adventure Course

Mt. Kilimanjaro, which in Swahili means "the white mountain," stands at an awe-inspiring 19,341 feet. At first glance, it appears that this towering structure with its three peaks—Kibo, Mawenzi, and Shira—has simply been placed on the surface of Tanzania's lush, flat landscape. Its isolation and singularity are the features that have earned it the title of the highest freestanding mountain on earth.

Mt. Kilimanjaro did not originate as a tourism destination

or an item on a mountaineer's bucket list. Instead, this world summit emerged as a volcano around 3 million years ago in conjunction with the formation of the Great Rift Valley. Of the three volcanic cones formed, Shira was the first to become dormant after its last eruption approximately half a million years ago. The Mawenzi cone was responsible for a large eruption that created the gorge found on the eastern rim, which also led to its extinction (KiliSummit 2001, 2010). The Mawenzi is connected to the highest cone, Kibo, via a ridgeline that forms the iconic saddle-shaped top of Kilimanjaro. It is on Kibo's crater rim that the highest peak, Uhuru Peak, is located at 19,341 feet.

It is also on the Kibo cone that visitors are able to get a breathtaking look at the crater and glacier that are unique to Africa's tallest mountain. Furtwängler Glacier is named after the German mountaineer Walter Furtwängler, who was among the fourth group to successfully summit Kilimanjaro in 1912 (Cullen et al., 2013). Scientists estimate that the Furtwängler Glacier has been present only since the early 1600s. Unfortunately, the glacier has seen significant reductions in size over the last 400 years. Historical records indicate that Earth's rising global temperatures have reduced the ice cover by 85 percent in the last century (Cullen et al., 2013). Additionally, it is predicted that no remaining ice bodies will be present on the plateau by 2040.

Although Mt. Kilimanjaro's early years were characterized by great volcanic activity and the formation of its now-famed features, the volcano is now classified as dormant. The last documented activity was 200 years ago and the last major eruption occurred a significant 360,000 years ago (Nelson, 2010). With the threat of eruption minimized, explorers began to view this towering structure as a feat to conquer. The earliest accurate accounts of climbing attempts date back to the 1860s. However, many attempts were likely made by locals or other travelers before the 1860s that were either never documented or were considered failed attempts. The first documented successful summit was by the German geologist Hans Meyer and an Austrian native, Ludwig Purtscheller, in 1889 (Peak Planet, 2019).

More recently, the primary purpose of the mountain has become focused on tourism as a source of income for Tanzania. Tourism earnings increased from $2.19 billion in 2017 to $2.49 billion in 2018, an increase of 7.13 percent (Dausen, 2019). The increase resulted from trekking groups leading numerous hikers up the mountain, as well as from the safaris and other natural attractions that draw visitors from around the world. However, although there are 50,000 visitors to the volcano a year, Tanzania remains one of the most impoverished countries in the world, ranked 183 out of 211 when comparing gross domestic product per capita (Dausen, 2019; World Population Review, n.d.). Mt. Kilimanjaro thus plays a significant role in maintaining Tanzania's economy and helping provide jobs for locals.

As tourism has grown, so has the accessibility of the volcano. Kilimanjaro now has seven routes: Marangu, Machame, Lemosho, Shira, Rongai, Northern Circuit, and Umbwe. All vary in length and difficulty, making the volcano more accessible to an array of ambitious travelers. The inclusion of multiple routes has also allowed the maximum number of hikers permitted on the mountain to increase and, in turn, has increased the revenue for hiking companies. Additionally, the various routes allow travelers to choose their experience and travel through unique ecosystems, sceneries, and climates.

Mt. Kilimanjaro Climate and Ecosystems

The isolated position of Mt. Kilimanjaro gives it a unique climate that is ever-changing throughout a hiker's ascent. Strong equatorial trade winds, elevation, and alternating dry and wet seasons present hikers with unpredictable and precarious conditions that can change by the hour. There are two distinct wet seasons, the most prominent being from April until July. A shorter rainy season occurs during November. The dry seasons are from July until October and again from December until the beginning of March (Mt. Kilimanjaro Guide, n.d.). Hikers are encouraged to plan their trips during the dry seasons to avoid the risks that accompany high rainfall, freezing temperatures, and other hazards.

As unpredictable as the precipitation is the temperature on the mountain, which varies depending on the season, altitude, and time of day. The Machame route begins at the Machame Gate, which is located only 5,718 feet above sea level. This low altitude means that temperatures at the commencement of the trip can fall within a warm range of 70 to 90 degrees Fahrenheit. However, as you make the slow trek upward, the temperature gradually declines. At the highest summit, Uhuru Peak, temperatures can reach chilling values of between 20 and -20 degrees Fahrenheit (Mt. Kilimanjaro Guide, n.d.).

Moreover, the addition of wind can quickly lower these already freezing temperatures. Preparing for the unpredictable weather created by Mt. Kilimanjaro is the most crucial step in ensuring a safe and enjoyable trek. The key thing to remember when prepping your clothing is to layer up and layer smart. You will find yourself starting the morning with four layers and gradually shedding them until you are soaked from the sweat generated by the sun's intense rays and the strenuous upward climb.

In choosing the Machame route we not only experienced a range of climates, but also had the unique opportunity to travel through five incredibly varied ecosystems on our way to Uhuru Peak. As we continued along the same trail, the landscape, climate, and flora and fauna slowly transformed around us.

Rainforest

The first ecosystem we encountered on our trek was the rainforest, located between the elevations of 6,000 and 9,000 feet. This biome is characterized by lush, thick moss draping over towering trees, covering every inch of the forest. Its low elevation results in the warmest temperatures we experienced on our journey, as well as the highest humidity. This ecosystem receives 90 inches of rainfall a year, the highest amount among all five environments.

The humidity and rainfall make hiking in this ecosystem difficult in places, as the compact dirt is often wet and slick. Many times we found ourselves relying on our hiking poles to stabilize us as we slipped and slid, often ending up with muddy backsides. Additionally, the thick, moist air increased our perspiration, soaking our first outfit with sweat. However, the scenery was straight out of a fairy tale and the sporadic sightings of exotic birds and monkeys made it worth all the mess.

Heath

The second ecosystem is the heath, found at 9,000 to 11,000 feet elevation. Here, the canopy begins to open and the vastness of the mountain's terrain becomes apparent. The shrubbery, grasses, and small trees are short enough to see over, so we all took a few moments throughout the hike to appreciate the views. Additionally, this low-standing vegetation added a new element to this ecosystem: wind. In this case, the breeze was welcomed, given that our clothes already had a stench to them from the previous day in the warm and humid rainforest.

In this ecosystem we began to see our progress, which was a great motivator when fatigue from the long hours of arduous climbing started to set in. The temperature in the heath is very erratic, ranging from 100 degrees to below freezing. There is less rain in this ecosystem, but instead there is frequent mist and fog, especially in the morning. On the Machame route, the heath hike is characterized by a steep climb up naturally formed rock step structures. The narrow path forced the group to travel single file up the rocky staircase in quick switchbacks, which gave us all time for personal introspection.

Moorland

The SpongeBob Tree (Dendrosenecio kilimanjari) is a giant groundsel found only on Kilimanjaro. These unusual plants can be seen around Barranco Camp.
Courtesy of the Tanzania Wilderness and Adventure Course

The third ecosystem is the moorland, found at 11,000 to 13,000 feet elevation. This ecosystem requires sunscreen, as this is when hikers start to climb through and above the clouds. It is a unique and breathtaking sight to look out and see clouds not only above, but also below. The triumph of passing the cloud line was a moment when we truly began to understand how far we had already come. However, the looming peak in front of us also served as a reminder of how far we had yet to travel. In the moorland, the small trees, grasses, and shrubbery begin to get shorter and disappear into short grass and rocks. There was also one particularly bizarre plant that our group christened the "SpongeBob trees" because of their cartoon-like appearance.

On this day, one of our fellow classmates woke up freezing,

as we all did, and decided to implement the layering technique and finally put her wool items to good use. She started by putting on wool leggings, followed by her hiking pants, and finishing with her rain pants, so as not to risk the unpredictable appearance of rain. Then we started upwards.

Thirty minutes into the slow ascent, she realized she was overheating. Although we had learned that gauging the temperature of the mountain was difficult, the heat we generated while hiking complicated the decision of what to wear. Starting at the front of the group, the girl in wool stopped and asked those around her to form a barricade as she removed her hiking boots (which is an effort) and stripped down to her Patagonia moisture-wicking underwear on the steepest incline. At one point she almost fell, but thanks to her human barricade, she was saved when her backside came into contact with another classmate's back. On the bright side, she did remember the rule of layering and was able to alleviate the problem without having to stop a porter to open up her duffel.

Alpine Desert

The fourth ecosystem is the alpine desert. As the name suggests, this is an almost alien terrain characterized by a barren landscape whose most prominent feature is large, dark volcanic rocks and boulders. At between 13,000 and 16,000 feet elevation, this region receives less than 8 inches of rainfall a year. The lack of rain results in a dry, cold, and windy climate with few plant species capable of surviving in the drought conditions. In fact, only three species of tussock grass have been found to survive in this arid terrain.

The temperatures reached below freezing at night, creating an eerily exquisite blanket of frost when we woke up. However, the frost quickly disappeared when the sun began to rise. At these now heightened elevations, the intensity of the sun doubles and is inescapable, and sunscreen is of even greater importance.

We also noticed the transition to a rocky desert, and the options for venturing off the trail for a luxurious outdoor bathroom experience became more limited. A few of our class members suggested that future hikers should keep their eyes peeled for an especially large or comfy rock, which can be a lifesaver when you begin to feel the generous amount of water you have drunk mixed with the Diamox medication.

When hiking in the alpine desert, it can seem like a lot of the same. It felt like we were seeing the same dark rocks for hours on end, at times causing us to suspect we were going in circles. What kept us going was remembering that it is all part of the journey and with each step, we were one step closer to the summit. While trekking through this terrain, as well as during our time in the others, we tried to take it all in for its originality and beauty, reminding ourselves of our purpose for climbing. Now more than ever, we began to feel greater determination and more pride in every step we took.

Summit

The final, most breathtaking, and unparalleled ecosystem is the summit zone. After the difficult journey up, all our expectations were exceeded when the first sliver of sunlight peeked over the horizon, finally giving us a glimpse of the end. The final hike to the summit required all of our remaining determination and strength. The eight-hour trek to Stella Point is done entirely in the dark, with only the feet of the person in front of us visible from our headlamp lights. Therefore, the majority of what we saw as we began to enter this climate zone was the gray, icy gravel at our feet.

The temperatures were especially low as we started our ascent, between 20°F and -20°F. We were encouraged to wear as many layers as we had brought with us. It was better to be hot and remove layers than to be freezing in the dark near the summit. However, as the sun eventually began to appear around the time we reached Stella Point, some layers started to come off when we began our descent back to our campsite.

It was not until Stella Point was in sight that we began to notice large patches of snow covering the desolate environment. Additionally, very little precipitation reaches this region of the mountain. The little rainfall that does occur is taken up and stored within the glacier.

Upon reaching Stella Point, we were greeted with a strong, chilling wind that swept through the crater and over the rim. From here, we walked west along the rim with the crater and glacier to our right. With the air especially thin, the temperatures below freezing, and the wind and icy surface threatening to push us off the lip of the mountain, the seemingly short distance of 1.5 miles to Uhuru Peak proved to be the most mentally and physically challenging feat yet.

Looking around, we were amazed by the shocking beauty of such an alien environment. The blanket of ice creates a rainbow of colors when hit by the sun's rays, and the sweeping view of Tanzania to the south and Kenya to the north provided us with a perspective that can be seen only from the roof of Africa. However, there are no signs of life in this environment. The low oxygen levels and erratic climate do not permit any species to survive at this elevation. The lack of life is what encourages you to get to Uhuru Peak and back down to a lower elevation as quickly as you can, because, as a guide perfectly put it, "Nothing lives up here, and neither can you."

At a whopping 16,000 to 19,341 feet elevation, the summit climate zone is one that few people in the world have the privilege of experiencing. Before reaching the ridgeline at Stella Point, we were slowly scaling up what is known as scree. Scree is loose dirt and gravel that is often found surrounding volcanoes and accumulates from rockfall or ash collection. Interestingly, it is the nature of this scree that inspired the 11 p.m. wake-up call that began our day. During the night, when temperatures are the lowest, the dew freezes around the scree and makes it almost solid. When frozen, the climb becomes reasonably manageable and there is little slipping and sliding.

However, after the sun has risen and you are on your way back to Barafu Camp, you no longer have the frozen scree providing a secure path down the mountain. The thawed-out scree is now loose, dry gravel, which loosens further with each step you take down the steep slope. As a result, you are likely to experience a lot of falls.

After feeling defeated multiple times by the scree, we learned to adopt a skiing-like technique in which we allowed our feet to slide *with* the scree, helping us to move faster and not end up with bruised behinds. It is also on your descent when you are likely to get scorched by the sun. Packing sunscreen for the summit might have seemed silly when we began our hike in the dead of night. However, when we reached Uhuru Peak, we realized that the sun has no mercy and without sunscreen we would have received our worst sunburn yet, likely in an odd shape depending on our choice of face covering. Sunglasses are also essential to prevent the reflective ice surface from blinding you. Skiing down to Barafu Camp still felt exhausting, but all of us knew we would get a couple of hours of sleep before descending down to our last campsite.

Chapter 4

The People of Kilimanjaro—
Indigenous Relationships

Nik Streit

Mt. Kilimanjaro is the highest freestanding mountain in the world, Africa's highest peak, one of the Seven Summits, and a major climbing destination for people worldwide. Kilimanjaro represents a unique travel opportunity and a once-in-a-lifetime experience for the thousands of trekkers who set out to climb it every year. Climbing Kilimanjaro is no easy feat; it is so difficult, in fact, that tourists who wish to do so require an extensive mountain crew to assist them.

The teams consist of Tanzanian guides, porters, and cooks, each with their own responsibilities and duties, all of which are essential if trekkers hope to make it to the peak. Guides, who are the most experienced and senior members of the team, are required to spend several years as porters before undergoing a training program offered by park authorities. Guides are the most hands-on members of the group, directly overseeing logistics, trekkers' welfare, and the climb all the way to the summit.

The porters of Kilimanjaro are the heart and soul of the journey. These dedicated men and women allow tourists to focus on the climb by carrying their equipment, extra luggage, and supplies for the camp up the mountain. The cooks are responsible for providing meals for the trekkers, a difficult task due to the elevation and the fact that they have to carry all the ingredients and cooking utensils up the mountain with them. Without the dedication of these hardworking people, many climbers' dreams of summiting Mt. Kilimanjaro would never become a reality.

To understand how these roles came about, it was important for us to learn about the history of the mountain and its relationship with the local people, beginning with the Chagga tribe. The Chagga are one of the most prominent ethnic groups in Tanzania and their history is intertwined with that of Mt. Kilimanjaro. The story of the Chagga begins when they settled on the slopes of the mountain following a series of migrations thought to have occurred around the eleventh century, likely absorbing the aboriginal peoples who had lived there previously.

The Chagga are one of the historically wealthier ethnic groups of the region, in large part thanks to the relatively mild climate and fertility of the land they inhabited. For thousands of years, the Chagga have relied on agriculture and thus have developed effective techniques for irrigation, terracing, and organic fertilization. Traditionally the Chagga relied on crops such as bananas, millet, and various vegetables, although this along with many other aspects of their culture would change during the late nineteenth century.

The Chagga people had long welcomed traders to the region, but as the nineteenth century wore on and colonialism spread across the globe, they saw an ever-increasing number of missionaries, travelers, and foreign representatives. Hostilities with these foreigners began to rise following Britain and Germany's decision in 1886 to split spheres of influence in East Africa. Kilimanjaro and the Chagga territory fell within the German protectorate and many of the chieftains began to resist colonial rule as it encroached upon their autonomy.

Nevertheless, by the turn of the century the Chagga had been subjugated completely and their new German colonizers imposed radical changes on their traditional ways of life. A new system of cash taxes forced the Chagga to begin working for the Europeans, from whom they could receive wages. A very small number of Germans effectively controlled the Chagga through their chieftains by expanding the power of those who cooperated and replacing those who did not.

As one of the first tribes to accept European missionaries, the Chagga were also among the first to begin converting to Christianity, and this Christianization of the Chagga was further accelerated by colonialism until the majority of the population identified as Christian. The introduction of Western religion to the Chagga also brought about several other changes: Western schools were built, Western medicine was introduced, coffee growing was instituted, and trade with outsiders was monopolized by Europe. All of these changes signaled an economic transformation for the Chagga people. Their Westernization gave them a major advantage over the other tribes, due to the advanced machinery and technology available to them. Even well into the twenty-first century, Arabica coffee grown on the fertile slopes of the mountain is one of Tanzania's most important exports.

Following the German colonization of the region, reports about Kilimanjaro began to make their way back to Europe. While the German Republic regarded the natural resources as the number one prize of the region, many Western geographers and explorers set their sights on reaching the peak of Mt. Kilimanjaro. Originally scholars dismissed reported sightings of a snow-capped peak south of the Equator as nonsense. However, that did not deter Hans Meyer, who would become the first man in recorded history to summit Kilimanjaro in 1889.

Meyer was a professor of colonial geography and saw the new territory as an opportunity to advance German nationalism and achieve fame and wealth. Fueled by German nationalism, Meyer believed that Kilimanjaro was destined to be conquered by a German, because they were the ones to "discover" it. Upon his arrival at the German colony of Tanganyika in Tanzania, Meyer discovered that he would not be the first to attempt the climb, as an American naturalist and an Austro-Hungarian count had both tried and failed to climb and measure the height of the mountain previously.

Meyer gathered what information he could from their failures and set off on his own with fellow German Baron Von Eberstein. Upon reaching 18,000 feet, Meyer encountered a problem that no longer exists today: the entire peak was covered by a glacier. To summit, he would have to find a way to navigate the 100-foot ice walls. But with the baron struggling due to altitude sickness, he decided to turn around and attempt to summit another day.

Meyer's second attempt to climb Kilimanjaro would prove to be even more unsuccessful than the first, though this time it was due to local politics. As Meyer set off on his two-week journey from the coast to the mountain, the Abushiri revolt broke out. Abushiri al Harthi was a farmer who united the local traders, who had long been taken advantage of by the Germans. The expedition represented an easy target for Abushiri and he took Meyer hostage. Although Abushiri killed many other Germans, Meyer was able to escape as a result of his wealth, as Abushiri needed money to fund his revolution and Meyer paid the steep sum required for his release. Eventually, Germany put down the revolt, which allowed Meyer to attempt the climb for the third time.

This time Meyer redesigned the expedition from top to bottom by enlisting the help of Ludwig Purtscheller, a world-famous Austrian mountaineer, and Yohani Kinyala Lauwo, a Chagga villager who would guide the expedition. On the way up the mountain, Meyer used a series of different camps that focused more on acclimating to the higher elevation, which also helped food and equipment be resupplied without much delay. Once they reached the glacier line, they established camp just below it and began to cut ice steps into the glacier. After hours of hard work they had carved a path through the glacier. They then spent another few hours trudging through deep snow to reach the rim of the crater.

At this point, the climbers were exhausted and decided to return to camp and attempt to summit another day. Three days later they set out again using the route they had carved out previously. After six hours of climbing, they reached the summit, where the crater that had been concealed for so many centuries revealed itself to them. Meyer and his team would go on to study the crater before descending the mountain, with his expedition lasting 16 days at over 14,000 feet.

Meyer's expedition proved to be a tremendous success and one that would have a lasting impact on Kilimanjaro. It would be another 20 years before the Kibo crater was climbed again, and his method of using different camps would be adopted by trekking companies in the future. Furthermore, some of the camps that Meyer established, such as the Lava Tower, are still used today; this was one of the sites we visited during our own hike.

Meyer passed away in 1929 and is honored by a plaque in Kilimanjaro National Park. Purtscheller, who died in a climbing accident, is still regarded as one of the greatest climbers of all time, with more than 1700 peaks to his name. Lauwo lived until he was 125 and was the mountain's most famous guide for more than 70 years. In 1989, on the one hundredth anniversary of the climb, he was honored as one of the first co-ascendants. The many porters who accompanied them on their journey were posthumously honored as well.

The people of Kilimanjaro have had a long and complicated relationship with tourists that persists even today. Kilimanjaro is a huge attraction for hikers around the world and this influx of tourism contributes greatly to the local economy. However, it also leads to the exploitation of the local population. In truth, the local guides, cooks, and porters are at the center of a ruthless price war, as trekking companies often cut corners to try to lower prices. When this happens, the porters are the first to suffer, as they are at the bottom of the food chain.

Apart from a few high-quality operations that employ a team of porters whom they rely on for all their climbs, most porters are not employed permanently. Instead, many porters rely on freelance work, often walking many miles to the national park gate hoping someone will be looking for porters. This leaves the porters with almost no leverage, as there are far more porters available to work than are needed. Moreover, many of them are desperate for work, as they rely on this income to support their families. Porters are extremely hardworking and dedicated people despite all of this, yet they still don't know whether they will receive a job each day.

To avoid exploiting the porters, there are numerous things potential Kilimanjaro hikers can do when planning their trip. The most important fact to understand is that cheap Kilimanjaro climbs come at the expense of the porters. Many porters don't have their own tents and equipment; a trekking company must provide these items for them, which costs money. Carrying the additional equipment up and down the mountain requires more porters, which also costs money. More porters mean more mouths to feed, which adds costs both for the food itself and to transport it up the mountain.

When you book a cheap Kilimanjaro trip, not paying porters fairly and overworking them are the first things companies do to cut costs, and while tourists might not notice it, their porters certainly will. On a budget climb, the porters rely solely on your tips for their income, and as such you are expected to tip more. However, most climbers are unaware of this expectation and as a result, the porters end up with less money.

Finally, it would be a mistake to assume that because a company is well known it treats its porters fairly. Some of the biggest companies are among the worst offenders when it comes to exploiting porters. Organizations such as the Kilimanjaro Porters Assistance Project (KPAP) have a mission of improving the working conditions of porters. They provide clothing free of charge to the porters, offer educational opportunities to the local community, and advocate for fair wages and ethical treatment by all trekking companies.

One of the best choices one can make as a climber is to book a trip with one of KPAP's partners, all of whom have been vetted to ensure that they are responsible and ethical trekking companies. KPAP is largely supported by donations from conscientious members of the climbing community. After we finished our hike and researched Kilimanjaro more for our academic work, we realized that the company we had chosen for our trek was not vetted by KPAP, and therefore not completely ethical to its porters or the locals we relied on to complete the climb.

This remains one of the main elements we would have changed about our trip. We all agreed that even if the trip had been slightly more expensive, we would rather have been certain that the porters were treated fairly and paid appropriately for their work. Other countries have exploited the locals for years, and we regret supporting a company that did not do everything in its power to treat the workers fairly. We strongly recommend that future hikers use KPAP as a resource when booking their trips.

Chapter 5

Day One: Machame Gate to Machame Camp

Kenny Sklar

Our long-awaited adventure began with a 7 a.m. wake-up the day we would start hiking. The group finished packing our daypacks and our larger duffel bags that the porters would carry and had one last breakfast at the hotel as the guides loaded up our large bus. It was a hectic morning, with everyone bouncing from getting food to making sure they had everything packed, especially water bottles. In the national park, plastic bottles are prohibited to keep the environment beautiful for everyone visiting now and in the future. Drinking lots of water on the hike is extremely important due to the rapid changes in altitude, the energy exerted while hiking, and the effects of the medication recommended for the hike. All hikers are advised to take some form of altitude medication to prevent the altitude sickness and severe headaches that can sideline anyone, regardless of their fitness level or training.

Everyone boarded the bus feeling giddy, with a healthy amount of both excitement and nerves. The entire bus was completely full, with everyone scrunched together, bags in our laps, and a few people sitting on the floor. The ride from our hotel to the bottom of the mountain took over an hour and everyone could not stop talking about our upcoming adventure. We also made conversation with our guides, who rode on the bus with us and answered any last-minute questions we had about the upcoming hike.

Once we arrived at Machame Gate, everyone who needed gear provided by the guide company, such as trekking poles and sleeping bags, quickly grabbed those items, while the porters organized the rest of the gear. It was a chaotic scene as we arrived, with all the guides and porters scrambling to get their own equipment and packs as well. It takes a lot of people to carry all the cooking and cleaning equipment, as well as the tents and their own belongings needed for the trek, which made us all appreciate that reaching the summit would be not just a personal accomplishment, but a collaborative group effort.

We then went over to the rest area and waited for our guides to bring our lunch. As we waited, we faced our first test. The rain started coming down and this change in the weather completely changed the mood of the group. The excitement drained away, not only among our group but for everyone at the gate. During this time we were stuck in a small space, trying to escape the torrential rain while random holes in the ceiling spewed water throughout the sheltered space.

We tried to play the types of games a camp counselor would suggest, like "Simon Says" and "Signs," in hopes of lifting the group's morale. The silver lining to the sudden storm was that we were better prepared for the weather going forward. Having our daypacks prepared for weather that could change in an instant was crucial and very useful during the rest of our trip, as we confronted many different types of terrain and countless changes in the weather.

We started to understand what the hike might look like because we would inevitably run into unexpected bad weather. As we waited, the rain continued to be strong and consistent, making us grow impatient for lunch. There was a small stand selling candy and drinks and it became a hot commodity for all the groups who were waiting for the rain to subside before beginning their hikes. We also started to raid the stash of snacks we had each brought along for the trip, which are a necessity to keep your energy up during the long time periods between meals.

After a long wait, lunch finally made it through the rain as it began to slow down. We had a boxed lunch assortment of chicken, crackers, and fruit. As we started to eat, the rain finally fully subsided and the sun poked through the clouds. As the sky cleared up, the rest of the mountain became visible. Our collective group spirit immediately soared.

A huge group of monkeys came up to us as we finished lunch, surprising us by stealing some bananas from a bunch sitting at the edge of the table. It was one of those moments that made us laugh uproariously, providing a funny story that all of us would forever connect to that day. It was also very special to see monkeys so close and after a while a few of us got the nerve to hand-feed them, even though this violated Leave No Trace practices. The monkeys were just a few feet away from us and would reach out and grab some of the leftover food from our lunches, as though they were asking, "You going to finish that?"

The final step before we began our journey was to register to enter the park and sign the communal log. Every hiker handwrites their signature and the date at each of the campsites, to track their progress and to make sure no one gets lost along the way. Once our whole group was registered, we started getting our packs on and preparing the proper rain gear in case it started to rain again. Then we began our long trek up the beautiful mountain.

The trail began on a wide road and at first we walked in large groups. Everyone started the hike walking very quickly, making it feel like we were racing to the top. The motto of the hike is *"pole pole,"* which means "slowly, slowly" in Swahili, but the first day we did not take that to heart.

For the entirety of the trip, one guide walked at the very front of the group to serve as the pacesetter for the journey. It was important to follow the guide's lead, both to assist with the altitude adjustment process as much as possible and to keep our progress at a steady pace so we would not burn out before the summit. Initially, however, members of our group did not follow that recommendation and trekked ahead of the pack enthusiastically.

As we continued, the path gradually narrowed from a road that could fit two cars to a small path that could fit only two people side by side. As the path became more constricted, the rainforest started to swallow us into the journey. Initially, as we walked through the gate, a sliver of sky illuminated the path ahead. But as the path narrowed in front of us the sun disappeared. Trees closed in above us until we were fully enveloped by the jungle and the rest of the brush around us.

The trail started at a very slight incline, barely enough to see, but after a long period of time we all started to notice the change in elevation. Kenny, a Colorado native, expressed concern that it was only the start of our journey and he was already wondering if this trip would be far too ambitious to handle. Despite his concerns, however, the only thing Kenny could do was continue to put one foot in front of the other and keep going.

The first day was full of energy. Everyone was getting to know our guides and asking questions about their experiences on the mountain and how they had gotten into the work of leading groups up Kilimanjaro. We played various riddle games to pass the time as we climbed, and we started to get into a good groove as we continued hiking on our first day.

Around halfway through the initial day, we arrived at the only rest spot along the trail that wasn't part of a camp. That became an issue on other days as we hiked long hours with no rest stop in sight. It was a good time to take our first longer break and prepare for the changing terrain ahead.

After the rest stop, the trail shifted from a consistent small incline to a wavy, very tight path that was much steeper and had roots that were used as steps at certain points. That was when the grind really started, foreshadowing how the rest of the long journey would go. The large steps were the first challenge to our quads, as we had to really stretch to get up some of the larger steps. At that point we were aching to see the camp through the trees, but the only relief we found was a small section of downward slope that put our legs back on reset mode.

A well-deserved group dinner after
reaching Machame Camp.
Courtesy of the Tanzania Wilderness and Adventure Course

During this time, some porters were flying by us carrying insane amounts of stuff with them. They would balance large bags on their heads or hold items like they were weightless; they seemed to have no trouble balancing large weights while hiking the uneven path. It was tremendously impressive, demonstrating how much strength and stamina they had developed as a result of the numerous treks that had made them seasoned veterans of the mountain. While we were out of breath and wheezing, they jogged past us yelling a friendly "JAMBO!"

Finally, after a strong first day on the mountain, we made it to our first camp. As we exited the jungle into an open space of rock with trees around the perimeter, everyone collectively sighed with relief as our first day was coming to an end. It was hard to anticipate exactly what the trail ahead would look like, but everyone was in high spirits and ready to tackle the rest of the journey.

Once we reached the first open area since leaving the gate we tried looking for the peak of the mountain, but it was hidden behind the clouds. It was daunting to have the peak seem so out of reach, and it reminded us that we had only one section behind us with a long way to go. We checked in at the office and signed in to track our group's movements, then headed toward where our group would spend the night. Although it was the slow part of the season when we made our journey in January, there were still a large number of tents set up and many people walking around the area. The campsite wasn't flat and we descended to a lower section where the porters had already set up our tents, including the larger tent that provided a place for our entire group to gather for meals and conversation.

Once we reached our group of tents we retrieved our larger packs and moved our belongings into our tents to get set up for our first night on the mountain. Then we all assembled in the larger tent, where we had our first meal of the adventure. It was very comforting to have a good meal after the first day, but as the days wore on and the intensity of the climb escalated, those dinners were not always so calm or comforting.

One of the most important aspects of the trip was getting adequate sleep. Pretty much every night on the mountain we tried to go to sleep as early as possible. You don't have a lot of extra energy for hanging out during the ascent. The first day had gone pretty well, with everyone making it to the first camp. Unfortunately, some members of our group were not feeling 100 percent. Although most of the group did not experience altitude problems, a few people had a challenging afternoon. This resulted in some group members asking the guides to carry their daypacks, moving slowly, and for one unfortunate individual, defecating in her pants as soon as she made it to the campsite. Although this was embarrassing, throughout the week we all had hard days, and we learned the importance of supporting one another through our struggles and giving ourselves grace on the days when we faced our greatest challenges.

Chapter 6

Day Two: Machame Camp to Shira Camp

Konnor Porro

Being in college is weird. We are all constantly trying to find a balance between being academically engaged and enjoying the social scene our university has to offer. Academics are the building blocks for the rest of our lives, yet we're advised to have as much fun as humanly possible during our college years, to inspire those crazy stories we can tell for decades. I have always found it difficult to live these two lifestyles simultaneously. Luckily, I have finally found a simple solution: climb a mountain.

Our climb combined these two goals brilliantly. Fun and work were naturally interwoven on Mt. Kilimanjaro. When we had to push ourselves to the limit, the feeling was one of ecstasy. Work and pleasure became one during life on the mountain. The hard work that hiking requires provided the foundation for stories we will share for the rest of our lives.

Day Two began with a beautiful sunny morning wake-up at the Machame Camp. The 6:30 a.m. start sounded daunting to college students at first, but falling asleep when it got dark and waking up with the sun felt much more natural than we could have anticipated. We also never fully adjusted to the Tanzanian time zone, which helped with the first early morning start.

Even before the guides came into our tents to make sure we were awake, most of us had already opened our eyes. With the mixture of excitement and anxiety that soon became our natural alarm clock, we all wanted to attack the day. Back home, having to wake up for an 8 a.m. class was one of the most dreadful moments each week, but this was different.

As the sun rose, we were already planning our journey for the day. This was no ordinary Tuesday where we started with our regular social media check. It was Day Two on Mt. Kilimanjaro—this was game day. Nothing else mattered besides finishing the day's climb and preparing for the next day.

We'd all had a strange night's sleep that first night, which could have been from the malaria pills or jitters from knowing it would be our first full day on the mountain. The Diamox also made us wake up to pee about five times a night, which is something any future Kilimanjaro hiker should be prepared for. This would be the first day where we would be on the mountain from dawn to dusk.

There was, however, an activity we all participated in each morning that helped calm our jitters. Morning stretching put our nervousness on pause as we engaged in our first movements of the day with our crew. Being in a new environment affects different people in different ways. Regardless of whether we were yogis or couldn't even touch our toes, we learned the importance of moving our muscles before starting each day on the trail. Stretching also helped alleviate the back pain some of us felt from sleeping on the ground.

After a nice stretch, there is nothing better than a full breakfast. The cooks, who doubled as porters, made up tasty meals, which always included bananas. These savory bananas became our friends on this adventure. Each morning we also held a quick award ceremony in which we anonymously voted on who had been the most inspiring member of our group on the previous day. The winner would carry a small stuffed giraffe with them on that day's hike. After we chose our day's honoree, we began to walk before the clock hit 8 a.m.

At this point, rhythms were starting to form, like how quickly we hiked, how chatty we were while walking, and how much water we consumed throughout from our hydration bladders. Everyone began to groove to each other's steps a little bit more.

We understood the smooth and consistent movement that the guides and porters used to guide the group. We also noticed just what superheroes these men and women became during our hike.

By carrying our heaviest bags, these locals allowed the climbers to fully embrace the beauty of the mountain. Their love for each other and the mountain was powerful and contagious. When things got tough, they were there for us. This trust and support became one of the most meaningful elements of the climb. The guides helped to mediate our relationship with the mountain. They showed us how to respect the mountain, even when things got difficult. The mountain gave off an energy that was transformed into deep, meaningful connection.

As we began to hike, our calves started to burn (if they hadn't already done so on Day One). Everyone had gained a firm understanding of *"pole pole"* by now, and we started to learn our lesson from tripping when we failed to watch our step or walking too quickly when it would have been more enjoyable to go at a slower pace. The trail from Machame Camp to Shira Camp is steep. The wet spots on rocks took down a couple of confident climbers, and it proved to be a humbling experience for us all.

When on the trail, everyone in our class became a meteorologist. Mornings might have clear skies after a night of howling winds. A day might start out cloudy yet end with a perfect sunset. Our ability to adapt to changes in the weather was critical, especially in the earlier days of the climb. Clothes eventually made the transformation from clean to sweat-stained, which became a norm for the trip. On this day our group was fortunate to have a beautiful sunny start to our morning, with some fog rolling in during the afternoon and a cool breeze to end the night.

There is an innate urge to move forward that we all felt while hiking. The satisfaction of successfully tackling each challenge made us feel more prepared to face the next one with confidence. Being able to wrestle with the day at a *"pole pole"* pace allowed everyone to peacefully experience Mt. Kilimanjaro.

On Day Two, our group split up a little bit, and that was okay. If we didn't feel like talking to people, we didn't. Some of us just watched in silence, alone with our thoughts as we took in the experience. Others played 21 Questions with each other. There were no rules. This was a time for each of us to find our groove.

We left the tropical rainforest environment and moved into a beautiful mountainous zone where the tall trees gave way to shrubbery. There were also some spots that provided easy rock climbing, and we learned to appreciate those moments. We walked at the pace that pleased us and we suggest that any future hiker do the same.

At this point in the trip, illness became inevitable for some. Taking in food and water became especially important, and we took advantage whenever there was a chance for a quick snack. However, for some this was easier said than done. Jack, a junior, was not feeling well on Day Two. He was absolutely drained of energy and nothing he ate would stay down. His stomach was turning when he woke up, but he *"pole pole*-ed" his way to camp that afternoon. All day, his stomach was empty and craving food, though his mind was repulsed by the idea of eating. But he did it. He took a prescription pill to keep his food down that night, and luckily this healed all wounds. Everyone has their own individual experience, and this was when Jack's strength was tested the most. Illness may set in, but it's nothing one can't overcome. Our collective strength inspired us all to keep going.

Our group became a family. When one person was down, we all felt down for them. We looked after each other as if we were siblings. It would not have been the same without each member of the group, and although most groups will be smaller than ours, I would bet every hiker feels the same.

Each climb has an individuality that cannot be duplicated. Everything that happened on the mountain became part of our group's story. For us, the bathroom situation was always a good conversation starter. Each bathroom story was crazier than the last. Day Two is when we felt more comfortable talking about these issues, as we almost all had them and expressing these small discomforts somehow overcame a barrier of shyness that we hadn't even realized was there. In a funny way, these friendships became more real after Day Two. That comfort among us remained for the rest of the trip. Bathroom talk became the norm, and some of our group's most memorable moments involved trying to squat over a hole. It's harder than it looks.

After a beautiful morning hike, we made it to Shira Camp. At this point, we were 12,467 feet above sea level. We knew that we were experiencing something special. We could feel the power of the mountain under our feet. We were now officially on mountain time, and we were adapting to mountain life.

Even with the yoga sessions each morning, the body is going to ache. The aches we felt became a rite of passage. We took pride in them.

At the base camp that afternoon, we had time to explore. We saw the cave where the original climbers once slept. We could finally see Uhuru Peak through the clouds. The clouds moved along the skyline and we became addicted to tracking their movements. A couple of us journaled or sketched what we were seeing, and the guides and porters gathered us around to sing us a song. When we journaled, we all had a feeling we were writing about similar themes of joy and simplicity. Our new goal was just to make it to the next day.

Chapter 7

Day Three: Shira Camp to Barranco Camp

Abby Fuller and Grace Jackson

For many of us, Day Three was the first time the hike got serious. Each of us began to realize how far we had already climbed and how much further we had to go in the coming days. Day One felt manageable because the first day's momentum and enthusiasm carried us as we walked quickly through the rainforest on our afternoon hike. Even though the guides kept cautioning us, *"Pole pole!"*, our excitement carried us to the first base camp with minimal difficulty. Day Two was another half day, and knowing we would be done hiking before lunch made it mentally manageable. Even though we climbed steep rocks and watched the environment shift to a more barren landscape, the anticipation of another short hiking day and our first full day on the trail continued to propel us all forward.

Facing Day Three of the six-day hike, in contrast, was terrifying. It was our first full day of hiking, with a lot of hard hiking days to follow. The idea of packing up after the rest we had enjoyed at the Shira Camp felt nerve-racking. Even though the collective group energy was high on Days One and Two, many of us had already experienced difficulties those first days due to the malaria medicine or our bodies reacting to the changing altitude. Now many of us felt a looming fear of what was to come.

We emerged from our tents sleepy, nervous, and once again not hungry due to the Diamox. Another round of crepes and porridge was served for breakfast and Kenny, the Colorado native, was again the only one who was able to eat a satisfying meal. After this quick breakfast and an exchange of fearful glances around the tent, we packed up our gear and began to line up. Our attire ranged from Summit Night max layers, with parka jackets and fleece pants, to trekking pants and long-sleeve shirts. Although it wasn't raining yet, the clouds signaled to us that the upward hike toward our lunch spot at Lava Tower would be difficult.

At breakfast, our professor, Rod, told us about his previous Day Three experience when he hiked Kilimanjaro for the first time. He recalled that it was indeed a difficult climb and warned us to apply sunscreen because Lava Tower would be above the cloud line, with a clear view of Uhuru Peak. For many of us, that was the goal that kept our feet moving forward when we could see nothing but an uphill slope ahead.

After about 20 minutes the rain began to come down: slowly at first, which prompted us to put on our rain jackets, then as a downpour, forcing us to stop and put on our rain pants and pack covers. It became difficult to talk to other members of the group, as we all had our heads down, focusing on our steps so we wouldn't be pelted in the face with freezing cold rain. This led each of us to spend a long time with nothing but our own thoughts. This was our first opportunity on the trail to reflect on the experience and allow our minds to wander. For some, this was incredibly taxing as they focused on their aching muscles and freezing bodies, but for others this provided some room to process what had happened over the last few days.

Day Three was also when many of us realized our rain gear was not as waterproof as we would have hoped. At first, the tiny droplets of water slid off our gear as advertised. But for those who had not invested in Gore-Tex, the droplets of water became less slippery and began seeping deeper and deeper into our layers of clothing until we became wet and cold to our core. That uncomfortably wet feeling would persist throughout the day until the warm afternoon finally arrived. This added physical hardship made the mentally difficult day even more challenging.

When we talked to one of the local guides, he explained to us that Day Three was typically his favorite, with full 360-degree views of the peak and the mountain below. Anticipating these views, which are featured by every travel brochure and hiking blogger, was initially what kept us going through a morning of uphill hiking that brought us to higher elevations than we had experienced before. But the harsh rain, which later turned to slush and then to snow, prevented us from seeing those views. What kept a lot of us going instead were the little moments of excitement, like when we stopped to dance with some of the porters to a Chance the Rapper song Cole was playing aloud on his phone, or when the guides sang us a song of encouragement after we had fallen into a prolonged silence as we engaged in our own internal monologues of quitting.

The morning hike ended at Lava Tower, but despite Rod's promise of sunshine and encouraging views, the rain was still pouring down. When we arrived most of the porters were taking shelter under overhanging rocks, while we were able to escape into our mealtime tent. This was another moment of introspection for some, as we realized what a significant class disparity we were experiencing throughout this journey. The porters had to hike to Lava Tower first, prepare our lunch, then huddle under the rocks for partial shelter.

Once we entered the tent, it was a struggle for many of us to remove our wet layers while maintaining internal warmth. Some of us reached into our bags only to find wet down jackets and soggy hand warmers. At our acclimation lunch at Lava Tower we were starting to experience the toll of the highest elevation yet. Many of us had difficulty taking in full breaths, which can be a scary experience if you have never been at an altitude near 15,190 feet, which most of us had never even come close to.

Our lunch was more banana and potato stew, which helped us take in more calories and bring our body temperatures back up. Although that should have been a meal we all wanted to scarf down, we found that meal to be one of the most challenging to eat due to the fact that we were freezing and experiencing the worst altitude sickness we had felt up to this point. As the meal ended and everyone exited the tent, the rain began to let up, and we could see the peak through the parting clouds. It looked so close that we wanted to just keep hiking up while we were so near, although in retrospect, we are all very glad that wasn't an option.

An important lesson we learned on that challenging morning was that synthetic layers were essential and a good raincoat could make or break your experience. Although no one can predict the weather for each group's climb, a rainy day at some point is almost guaranteed. The temperature changed drastically between morning and evening, so being able to change quickly also became extremely important.

Synthetic layers weren't just a matter of comfort but also became a matter of safety. If you didn't have them and inevitably became drenched from a downpour on a day like this, you would still have wet clothes the following day, when it would be even colder. Although shelling out money on gear for the trip may be painful, on days like our Day Three you will be thankful that you opted for a slightly pricier but more durable rain jacket and rain pants.

After taking some pictures as the clouds began to part, we slowly gathered our things and formed another single-file line. This time, instead of anticipating another half day of climbing uphill, we crossed the camp and looked through a canyon of rocks at the downward direction we would be hiking for the remainder of the day. We do this so our bodies can get a taste of the altitude and acclimate a little more without having to stay at that elevation for an extended period of time. Although downhill hiking takes a different toll on your body, our collective spirits were beginning to rise from the sun shining down on us and our increased ability to breathe again.

The first 30 minutes of the hike downhill consisted mainly of us taking calculated steps onto rocks and holding on to our peers and guides as we made the tricky descent into the canyon. This slower pace and controlled movement felt fun for some but somewhat terrifying for others. This section of the descent was our first real experience with walking downhill for longer periods of time and was the first point where perceived versus actual risk came into play. Although some steps felt a little less safe, we had to trust that we would not be placed in a dangerous situation and that the guides and our peers would be there if we fell. This section of the hike involved an element of fear, but as we gained confidence and passed through the steep downhill section, the day turned into a lot of fun.

As the weather improved and the path became clearer, we were finally able to take in the incredible views we had been promised earlier on. Although our excitement was likely due to the contrast with the gloomy morning, that afternoon was one of the best hikes yet. The warm sun dried our rain-soaked packs and provided us with an easy downhill hike, giving each of us an opportunity to embrace the time we were spending on this life-changing trip.

We started talking to each other again and that stretch of hiking was when many of us began to feel that we were growing closer to one another. We found it easier to slip into the deeper conversations that we were all encouraged to engage in from the beginning of the trip. After that hard morning of hiking, having overcome our first real collective hurdle, we had a little more confidence that we could get through the trip. Through that challenging experience we also learned to only let ourselves think about the hike in smaller stretches. In addition, as a result of our Day Three experience, a new team mentality began to emerge among the group.

We witnessed the terrain begin to change again, which felt

less exciting on the downward stretch because we knew we would be hiking back up from a different angle the next day. The landscape began to shift from sandy slopes and desert-like landscapes to twisty green trees and rivers that felt similar to our Day Two experience. It was comforting to see the change in the environment and know we would be sleeping in a place that felt more familiar and vegetated, unlike the barrenness of Lava Tower. But it was also anxiety-inducing to know we would be returning to the difficult and unfamiliar sights we had just encountered.

As we continued to hike, we saw the village of tents that marked the Barranco Camp below, which turned our calculated steps into an almost-run that felt a little bit reckless and out of control. Approaching our mealtime tent and seeing our gear laid out on tarps was one of the happier moments of the journey as we reached the end of a physically and emotionally challenging day. That was the first time we had to work on our mental strength. When many of us looked back later at our notebooks we saw the words "I am strong" repeated throughout our scribbled thoughts of the day, capturing the day's difficulties.

Even though the Barranco Camp was at 13,044 feet, which felt like only a minor upgrade from the Shira Camp's 12,500 feet the night before, we could still rest satisfied that night knowing we had accomplished something mentally difficult. The acclimation of Day Three wasn't preparing us only for the physical part of the Summit Night. It also served as an emotional preparation for Summit Night that we wouldn't even know we needed until that time came.

That evening we talked about our anticipation of the summit. Some of our group began to question whether they would be able to complete the hike. Although some of us were struggling with the altitude more than others, after finishing our third day of hiking, we all began to realize just how much we had completed, which gave us some encouragement for the long treks still to come.

As we left the tent after another dinner of stew and rice, we saw a beautiful sunset that contrasted with the looming Barranco wall we would have to climb tomorrow. Recalling the lesson we had learned from hiking on Day Three, we didn't let ourselves dwell on the challenge ahead. Instead, we congratulated ourselves for our day's accomplishments and rested up, knowing we would have another long day of hiking tomorrow.

Chapter 8

Day Four: Barranco Wall to Barafu Camp

Kelly Reimer

Day Three was a physically tough day due to a morning hike in the bitterly cold rain, snow, and fog followed by an afternoon hike down steep, rocky, and unsteady terrain. That day also brought to light which students were struggling consistently with the altitude and the persistence to carry on. We instructors spent some time with those students that evening to talk through their physical, mental, and emotional state. We also talked with the guides to make sure we were providing the right support and encouraged all the students to prepare them for Day Four. Our evening time together included encouragement, prayer, and some sharing of snacks, prompting a student who had not eaten much since Day One to comment, "Sweet Tarts are my favorite snack."

On Day Four, we awoke early, ate breakfast inside our blue dining tent (which gave everything, including our food, a bluish hue), and gathered up all our belongings. Our campsite overlooked Moshi, the town where our hotel was located. It was a refreshing start to the day to have a visible reminder of how far we had come and to remind the students how much we had already accomplished.

We started the day's hike with some gentle downhill climbs that took us over a small, wandering stream. Looming before us, though, was the Barranco Wall, a steep 843-foot wall that was both massive and daunting. As we approached the wall, we could feel the jitters and uncertainties of yesterday begin to return.

Fortunately, the Barranco Wall is not a sheer cliff or a

technically challenging climb. No special equipment is required to conquer this wall, and the guides know which path to take to allow for a slow and safe ascent. This climb is a full body workout—your legs support you in taking large steps as you head upwards through many switchbacks on rocky ledges, while you use your hands to steady yourself and pull yourself up over large rocks.

This was the one time we were encouraged to put our hiking poles in our daypacks and not use them at all. You need all four limbs to be in contact with the ground for this scramble up the wall. This portion of the climb is done in a single-file line. It takes mental energy and attentiveness to evaluate your next move, consider how you want to approach a large step, determine which portion of a ledge you want to grab hold of, follow carefully behind the person in front of you who is one step ahead, and encourage the person behind you to follow the step you just made.

Our guides stationed themselves along particular areas of the wall to provide guidance in the techniques needed to navigate each portion of the climb. The climb was methodical and slow, as different sections took varying levels of care to climb. Meanwhile, the porters whizzed past us, navigating the same terrain with ease while also carrying duffel bags, cooking supplies, water jugs, and more.

The most dangerous part of the wall is the "Kissing Rock," a narrow section of the trail with a drop-off that requires extra attentiveness. The name comes from the need to hug the wall so tightly that you can kiss it while taking a perilous step. Our guides were right there with us, providing step-by-step instructions and offering an outstretched hand to help us navigate each step. While the experience was intense, it was so different from our other hiking on the mountain up to that point that many students found it a fun and different kind of challenge.

After about a two-hour climb we reached the top of the Barranco Wall. Every student navigated the wall successfully, which was a huge achievement. At the top we were treated to a gorgeous view of the Barranco Valley and Mt. Meru. We took some time to rest, check in with each other, eat some snacks, and take a few photos with our guides.

The group takes a break at the top of the
Barranco Wall...perseverance!
Courtesy of the Tanzania Wilderness and Adventure Course

Shortly after arriving at the top of the Barranco Wall, our guides instructed us to get our hiking poles back out, put on our packs, and continue the journey. Our next destination was the Karangu Camp, where we would eat lunch. The next few hours were arduous. The landscape was barren except for small shrubs and scrubby trees. The clouds rolled over us, covering the landscape with grayness. The terrain was rocky, with lots of gravel, and the elevation continually changed as we went up and down hills.

When we rested to get water or just took a minute to sit down, we were able to look back across the landscape and see how far we had traveled. We could see people behind us who looked tiny in the distance amid the massive landscape. Our guides continued to encourage us and lead the way, even carrying our packs to lighten our loads when we thought we might not make it.

At one point during this journey, we saw many porters coming down the mountain with empty water containers, then passing us again going back uphill with water. One of our guides informed us that behind us was the last fresh water source on the mountain, so any water needed for meal preparation at Karangu Camp and Barafu Camp, as well as the water provided to hikers, had to be retrieved from this lower elevation. The porters who were responsible for water would make the journey down to this lower elevation multiple times for two days to ensure that groups had the water they needed.

As we approached the Karangu Camp we spotted our blue dining tent and felt a sense of relief that we had made it that far. The morning had been tough, but lunchtime gave us an opportunity to rest, drink some hot water, and get some sustenance to boost our energy.

We still had a few hours to hike after lunch, so our guides got us back on the trail again. With the constant cloud cover, we were ready for rain and it was cold, but once we got moving we warmed up again. The terrain changed to even more rock and there was no plant life at all.

The higher the altitude, the colder it got. We began adding layers of clothing throughout the afternoon ascent. Many of us imagined that this must be what the surface of a distant, desolate planet would look like. The entire journey after lunch felt uphill… perhaps because it was. In addition, several people experienced altitude sickness, as well as flu-like symptoms. We rested when we needed to and took slow, methodical steps—*"pole pole."*

When we arrived at Barafu Camp, we were overjoyed. The clouds parted and we were greeted with a beautiful blue sky. Smiles abounded at the sense of accomplishment, the hurdles we had overcome, the resilience we had developed, and the perseverance that would be rewarded with a hot meal and time to rest. As an instructor, I was incredibly proud that every student had made it to the base camp of Mt. Kilimanjaro. We stood at 4673 meters (15,331 feet). We had only made it that far because we had taken one step at a time, supported and encouraged each other, and been accompanied by amazing guides who believed in our abilities even when we struggled to believe in ourselves.

Chapter 9

Instructors' Reflections and Lessons Learned

Kristen Aquilino, Rod Parks, and Kelly Reimer

Three instructors accompanied the students on this journey. These are some reflections and lessons learned that we hope will be helpful to others.

Pre-Journey

- *Hire a trusted trekking company and trust your guides:* Working with a trusted trekking company is crucial to your journey. You need to feel comfortable with the company and its guides. You need to be able to lean on them for their expertise and guidance, especially when physical health concerns or emergencies arise while you are on the mountain.
- *Hold a gear check:* One evening, the instructors brought their gear to class to show it to the students. This gave the students an opportunity to ask questions, identify gaps in their own packing list, and discover where they might have too much gear. We followed up several days later by having the students bring in their own items for a gear check. This allowed time for the students to do last-minute shopping before we departed for Tanzania. The trekking company also had a gear check at the hotel the day before the trek, and some students ended up renting gear.
- *Get to know your co-instructors:* Knowing your co-instructors, the roles you each want to take on, and how you will communicate while traveling is crucial. Since we work at the same university, we knew each other through committee

work. But planning for the course, having some meals together, and hiking together periodically helped to build these relationships even further.

- *Encourage students to prepare physically:* Offer opportunities to hike together and work out together.

During the Trek

- *Encourage the students to build relationships with each other:* Students were asked to tent with someone different each night of the journey and to hike with different people. This helped expand their social circle throughout the journey.
- *Check in with students regularly in small groups and individually:* Every student handled this journey differently. Some bounded up the mountain and stayed at the head of the pack the whole time. Some took *"pole pole"* to heart. Some struggled physically and some mentally. Every student (as well as each instructor) had good days and bad days, and a check-in from an instructor can go a long way. Work with your co-instructors to assess how students are doing as a group and individually, then strategically reach out to students as needed.
- *Find balance for yourself:* Despite your responsibility for supporting the students, you also need to take care of yourself physically, mentally, and emotionally. All three instructors were sick at some point during the trek. We each had more or less to give of ourselves during those times. Depend on your co-instructors and lean on one another for support.
- *Cherish the journey:* You may be experiencing the journey for the first time, along with the students. Find time each day to reflect and journal. Enjoy the journey, and experience it through the eyes of your students as well.
- *Take it a step at a time:* Each day will bring something new:

a new challenge, a new celebration, a new illness, a new success. Just like climbing the mountain can only be achieved one step at a time, treat the entire journey and leading the students the same way—one step at a time.

Chapter 10

Summit Night

Jack DiPietro, Abby Fuller, Nathan Jones, Liam Lindy, and Carson White

The Night Before

We reached Barafu Camp on our fourth day on the Machame Route on Kilimanjaro, arriving there after a tough day of hiking from Barranco Camp through Karangu Camp. The hiking conditions we experienced could not have been more different from those we had encountered the day before. Our acclimation hike up to Lava Tower developed our mental toughness, physical stamina, and ability to adjust to the high altitudes. Had we not lived through Lava Tower and the other hard days that preceded Summit Night, we would not have been able to arrive at Barafu Camp—the site where we would rest before the final ascent to Stella Point and finally to Uhuru Peak.

Most of the group had acclimatized well, but a couple of people weren't as lucky. We all struggled with the altitude at certain points, but a few of our class members seemed to experience a different level of energy loss and discomfort. These class members were the ones who made Barafu Camp their peak. For the six-day route, the success rate of hikers making it to the peak is about 65 percent, meaning that while we were hiking, we had to live with the knowledge that we might not all make it to that famous sign we had been hoping for.

Additionally, males aged 18–35 are among the least likely to make it to the top, because they tend to be overly confident in their physical ability and do not take *"pole pole"* to heart. While it would have been statistically improbable for all of us to reach the summit, it was still disappointing for the one instructor and two students who opted not to attempt the summit hike due to altitude sickness. Nevertheless, their resilience in facing this disappointment brought new meaning to the phrase "mental toughness."

For the first three days, we hiked in two 13-person groups, a faster group and a slower group, to accommodate people's preferences for different paces. However, on the fourth day, particularly in the afternoon, we dispersed into smaller groups of four or five, which was a nice change. During this time we were each able to pause and check in with ourselves, reflect on how we were doing, and spend time thinking about things that often get pushed to the wayside during a busy semester. Spending time alone on the trail in silence was important for all of us. We would all recommend to others to arrange time for that kind of silence, and not to always fill it with a playlist or a podcast.

Being alone with ourselves for a couple of hours was a gift as it allowed us to get our minds in order before starting the process of trekking up to the summit the next morning. During this time, Liam, a computer science major obsessed with the brand Patagonia, thought about how blessed he was to be there, to be able to take a week away from his busy life, and to have instructors who were able to make all this happen. He felt gratitude for the guides and porters, for his parents who encouraged him and financially supported the endeavor, and for his own physical health.

This was a good moment for all of us to practice gratitude and reinforce in our own minds how amazing this experience was, even before we even reached Uhuru Peak. Although we didn't have perfect weather for our climb, Liam remembered the guidance, "You have to weather the storms on the way up to enjoy the view on the mountaintop." While the advice may sound clichéd, it felt extremely applicable in this context.

We transitioned to the alpine desert, a climate with very

few plants where the trail becomes looser stone, although not the piles of rocks you encounter when you reach the more serious altitudes. At this point we really took *"pole pole"* to heart, maintaining a slower pace. This experience was a good reminder for us because in college, and in life in general, we're often going a thousand miles a minute. While in the moment we may think all this rushing around is worth it, when we finally arrive at whatever our destination is, we frequently realize that going super-fast was not the best idea.

After taking it easy for most of the day, Liam walked into Barafu Camp with a feeling of ease and the realization that, "Yes, I can do this!" This was an important lesson that going fast is not always best. Although Liam felt invigorated, however, many other members of the group remembered feeling physically very drained and stressed about how they would have enough energy to complete their hike to the summit.

Once we reached Barafu Camp we were ready to settle in for Summit Eve. This was kind of like Christmas Eve in the sense that we were waiting with great anticipation for something we knew was just around the corner. However, this time was also filled with dread, because we were unsure of what the next day would bring and whether we would all make it to the top.

We arrived at the camp at about five o'clock feeling ready to eat dinner, have some tea, and go to bed. Ultimately that did not occur, and in hindsight we were grateful for that. It took quite a while to work out all the logistics of the evening and we ended up eating dinner a bit later than the guides had planned, but this trip was all about expecting the unexpected. This delay forced us all to talk with each other about the day and really catch up. At this point we were past engaging in small talk, as we had been on the trail for four days and had spent time together regularly for about 14 days, between being in class stateside, traveling to Tanzania, and being on the trail.

While we usually had these times together each evening in

between settling into camp and when the meal was ready, that night at Barafu Camp was different. Normally, each day we would get into camp, unpack, briefly nap for a bit, then talk; however, it had still been a lot of small talk up to this point. This night marked a turning point in the dining tent conversation.

Since this was a Wilderness and Adventure Therapy course, before we left for Tanzania we had discussed the "masks" we wear, the emotional barriers we put up in order to fit in and protect ourselves from vulnerability. In each hike we all had moments of vulnerability and progress, but in the dining tent that night many people's masks came all the way off. We all became more emotionally vulnerable and open. This is why we gave this night its own designation: Summit Eve.

It was at this point that we as a group could sense that "It" was near: the summit, Uhuru Peak. Because we faced something so physically challenging, we had no choice but to let our guard down and be vulnerable with one another. When doing something so strenuous, it is impossible to continue hiding weakness. That was a recurring theme with Barafu: the nearness of the summit could be felt with anticipation.

We had a great dinner that night. It was a rice and vegetable stew and even though none of us particularly had an appetite, we were getting used to the rhythm of eating purely for energy's sake. Even though the altitude medicine took away our appetites, we knew it was important to eat anything that we could keep down, so it was a big accomplishment when many of us finished our meals that night.

After dinner, the guides came into the dining tent to do their medical rounds, as they routinely did every night after dinner, checking our resting heart rate and other vitals. That night they gave off vibes that they were being more stringent at this particular check-in, although these checks, at least for our group, felt like a formality, mainly because people either knew they were doing well or knew they were not. Even though Barafu

Camp would be the peak for at least three of our members, reaching this point was no small achievement. That evening our professor, Rod, spoke about his experience on Summit Night when he previously hiked Kilimanjaro in the summer of 2019. He stressed what a significant accomplishment it was to reach Barafu. When we all ate dinner together that night, we knew that to be true.

After our medical checks we all went to bed as quickly as possible, because it was pushing 8 p.m. and we knew that 11 p.m., the wake-up time for our final hike, was rapidly approaching. It is important at this point to note that in Swahili, the native language of Tanzania, the word Barafu means ice, or having to do with ice. This is an entirely fitting name because it is very cold at Barafu Camp, which is located in the fifth and final zone, the Summit Zone, of Mt. Kilimanjaro. Whereas on most other nights we slept warm with our insulated sleeping bags, on Summit Eve we struggled to fall asleep because of the cold and our inability to get a full breath of air due to the lack of oxygen. Some of us remembered waking up from our sleep out of breath just from rolling over. While some people were exhausted and passed out immediately, others could not fall asleep in anticipation of the difficult hike that was so near.

Breakfast and a Tale

On January 16, 2020, 21 of us were woken up by a porter at 11 p.m. to begin climbing the final 4,102 feet of Mt. Kilimanjaro. The night was cold, but vaguely noticed due to our excitement about the climb.

With our headlamps on in the darkness, we put on our final pieces of apparel and loaded our packs for the climb. We were thankful we had taken the time to pack before our nap — sleeping for three hours cannot possibly be called anything more than a nap. Though we were exhausted upon our arrival at Barafu Camp, waking up to our bag prepped and ready to go saved time and calmed our anxiety about whether we had everything we needed for that morning.

For the purposes of the next seven hours of the hike, our primary concern was weight. Up to this point, the climb had been manageable with a daypack that could weigh up to 15–20 pounds, depending on our individual provisions. During Summit Night, however, a 20-pound bag would soon feel like 70 pounds as we exerted ourselves more and became more oxygen-deprived. Bare essentials were all that was needed—we promise. Aside from the clothing on our bodies, the next heaviest object we carried was water. Other important items included a few lightweight snacks, such as granola or power bars. During the climb, we had a couple of short opportunities to refuel our bodies and it was critically important to take advantage of them. Thoughtfully preparing your equipment will help maximize your chances of successfully summiting Mt. Kilimanjaro.

With our equipment in order, it was time to assemble in the dining tent. At this point, climbers brought their hydration reservoirs and water bottles to be filled with freshly boiled water by our wonderful porters and guides. We walked into a dim tent full of exhausted but excited faces. We sat around a folding table adorned with various teas, drink mixes, trays of popcorn, and tea biscuits.

The insulated tent away from the wind offered a safe haven from the frigid temperatures outside. It was of paramount importance for climbers to eat and drink during this time, even if our stomachs were telling us otherwise. We knew our bodies were about to undergo hours of exertion with virtually no opportunity to recover. In the tent, we tried to eat the provided snacks and drink plenty of warm fluids. This was the last opportunity to warm our bodies, hydrate, and energize ourselves before what would surely be one of the most challenging nights of our lives.

As we spent time preparing our bodies for the challenge ahead, two of our classmates, Carson and Bailey, had brainstormed days before how we could also prepare our minds. What this meant was galvanizing our group and boosting our morale in the face of the intimidating task before us. They prepared a short, interactive, pump-up activity to lift the group's spirits and elicit a few laughs. Inspired by a viral video titled "An Irish Tale," the two students had created "A Tanzanian Tale."

A Tanzanian Tale: An Original Tale by Bailey Honig and Carson White

Ladies and gents, today is the day we do what we came here to do: fucking summit Kili!

We're gonna have to freeze our asses off to get there... *(crowd sighs)*
Good thing we got fat asses! *(crowd cheers)*

Diamox made me lose feeling in my feet... *(crowd sighs)*
But Rod gave me a foot massage! *(crowd cheers)*

I think I might have malaria; my meds didn't work... *(crowd sighs)*
The wet dreams were worth it! *(crowd cheers)*

Timmy's neck is still red from the safari... *(crowd sighs)*
The locals love it! *(crowd cheers)*

TSA took away my pocketknife... *(crowd sighs)*
So I bought a spear at the gift shop! *(crowd cheers)*

Cole took a shit in our bathroom... *(crowd sighs)*
So we cut his electricity! *(crowd cheers)*

My shit bag is full... *(crowd sighs)*
Good thing I brought an extra! *(crowd cheers)*

This tale is making it hard to breathe... *(crowd sighs)*
Good thing we're fucking done! *(crowd cheers)*

"A Tanzanian Tale" turned a quiet, tired, and anxious tent of climbers into one full of laughter and excitement. This was one of the most memorable moments of the climb. Something as simple as a comical speech rallied our group, and suddenly people who were extremely nervous became eager for the challenge.

The Challenges of Summiting

With our heads facing straight down, watching our legs move in a repetitive motion, we struck out in a single line, focused on a cadence that would get us to the top. Things were very still at this point and you could hear every breath being taken. About 15 minutes into the hike, we began to hear faint moans and cries that grew in volume as we approached a fellow hiker who was off the side of the trail, bawling their eyes out and throwing up what appeared to be blood. We all thought to ourselves grimly, *Wow, what a comforting feeling, knowing we've barely even gotten started with this 10+ hour venture ahead.* This was a great reality check for the group and also a moment of compassion, remembering the hikers in our group who were not as lucky to be hiking up the mountain this morning.

Visually, this experience was unforgettable. Peering up the mountain and seeing other trekkers' headlamps scattered all along the trail to the top was absolutely daunting. "We'll be there soon," we kept telling ourselves.

As our eyes began to adjust to the darkness, the stars glistened with light and occasionally we would see a shooting star, imbuing us with slightly more hope. Our group's spirits remained high, with a few people listening to music and feeling the rhythm. Unlike the other days of climbing, something was significantly different about tonight: absolute silence. No words were spoken and there was no conversation whatsoever, just the very quiet music.

The unique thing about this was that we had never felt more unified and united as a group, despite the silence. We were all completely focused on conserving our energy and overcoming the extreme challenge we confronted. Each break we took early in the hike was very brief to ensure that our muscles remained warm and prepared. Carson, one of the fittest and most positive members of the group, didn't want to stop at all, knowing it would just delay us from reaching our destination. Others, however, welcomed any opportunity they had to stop and regain some sort of energy.

"*Pole pole*" signifies that each of us can summit the mountain in our own time, as long as we recognize the balance our bodies need, and as long as we recognize that each of our bodies is different and needs different things. While trudging slowly up Kilimanjaro, the group heard a fellow hiker from another group cry out in anguish, pleading with their partners to be taken back down. To our right, there was nothing but rock silhouetted in darkness.

The wind came piercing through this open landscape, penetrating every one of our layers and moving through us like a spirit. Ahead, one of our classmates experienced intense altitude sickness, able to take only a couple of steps at a time before needing to rest and catch their breath again. Nate offered them some water, taking the opportunity to rehydrate himself as well.

We heard a nearby guide utter "*pole pole*" to uplift a fellow student plagued with fear and exhaustion. Hearing this helped contextualize the isolation of our individual struggles, enabling us to center our own experience as a necessary part of a collective struggle toward something bigger than ourselves. Far off in the distance, beyond the false summits that taunted us along the way, the peak awaited our arrival.

After another hour of treacherous hiking, we tossed our bags down to eat nibbles of Clif Bars for energy and drink the water that was quickly freezing in our Camelbaks. We all felt the summit was close, but we could not quite see it yet.

Each member of our class recalled not necessarily expecting to summit Mt. Kilimanjaro. We had all been told multiple times that the success rate was not 100 percent and things like altitude sickness were relatively out of our control.

That night, the stars persisted to light up the mountain, all of us drawn to gaze upward as we continued to hike. Each time feelings of discouragement or doubt began to invade, we took a deep breath and found peace beyond the sky. We just needed to take one step at a time.

As the night went on and the weather intensified, the hours began to blend together. Discomfort in our joints, the cold and wind, and mental fatigue began to set in as we navigated this perilous terrain. The visible crest of the Reusch Crater, a volcanic crater that looks alarmingly like a giant hole in the ground, seemed to be permanently affixed out of reach. With every step, Stella Point and Uhuru Peak seemed to stretch further out of our grasp. At this point in the climb, we realized just how strenuous the journey was. We could either embrace discomfort and move forward or accept failure in summiting Mt. Kilimanjaro.

All climbers reach this moment. Jack, the redhead who decided to wear tennis shoes instead of hiking boots, confronted this thought approximately 30 minutes from Stella Point at roughly 18,000 feet. He had prepared in seemingly every way possible for the challenge, but there is no simulation for the mental and physical discomfort he encountered. Underneath two pairs of insulated ski socks, he began to feel his toes seize in the cold. His fingers soon followed as temperatures plummeted unrelentingly to -20°F. His ankles, knees, and lower back were on fire with aches and pain from the continuous impact. Worst of all, he was confronted with the prospect of failure.

Jack reached a moment where he became lost in the repetition of putting one foot in front of the other. As the challenge of the climb faded into mindless marching up the mountain, he began to contemplate what would happen if he stopped walking. This was a moment each of us had, even though it sounds crazy to contemplate quitting so close to the end of the summit hike.

We had what felt like an infinite amount of time to be present in our thoughts. These thoughts spanned everything from existential queries to past and present relationships. But the most profound thought we could muster was a feeling of insignificance and isolation. These thoughts did not present themselves in a negative light but were instigated by the beauty and scale of our surroundings. As we trekked under millions of stars and the glowing Milky Way, we couldn't help but feel beautifully infinitesimal and alone.

The mountain whose summit we neared with every step was the single largest *thing* any of us had ever encountered. It was the largest mass, object, ecosystem, and challenge we had ever ventured or undertaken. Our class felt alien, and rightfully so, to this environment. Its beauty and power were overwhelming.

All the while, our class, which had now grown exceptionally close, trudged forward single file in silence. There wasn't enough energy for conversation. Everyone had delved into their own thoughts and sought their own means of continuing forward. We were only a few feet apart but could have been miles away from each other. We were on our own.

There is absolutely no way for a climber to subject themselves to these conditions and not experience discomfort. Hours of exposure at this altitude and continuous physical exertion will take its toll on the mind and body. This is where climbers who complete the trek "embrace the suck." In other words, they find a way to become comfortable with being uncomfortable. There is no true way to prepare for this experience without prior trekking experience at this level or altitude. However painful, exhausting, and at times unbearable these moments are, they are also the moments that truly define your experience. These memories validate the effort, bumps, bruises, and time invested in the journey.

As the sun slowly began to rise, we reached Stella Point. To celebrate, our guides gave us warm beverages to keep our body heat up and to serve as a small reward. The most amazing part of this moment, besides the sunrise, was that everyone seemed to forget about Uhuru Peak, the site of the famous Kilimanjaro sign. Stella Point could have been a false summit. It could have been demoralizing and frustrating. Instead, it was beautiful and worthy of celebration. It was one of the freest moments we experienced throughout the entire trip.

The Summit

After taking a quick celebratory break at Stella Point, we knew we needed to keep going. The snowcaps were finally coming into sight, which was a sign we were getting close to the top — or at least it felt like it. The edge seemed at every moment to be just an arm's length away; however, each time you looked up at it, you felt as if you were just as far away as the last time. It was a constant mind game of wanting to give up but forcing yourself to push through because you were finally this close.

At about 5:30 a.m. we began to see the earliest stages of light and sunrise projected across the horizon. The sun wasn't actually visible yet, but you could tell it was making progress as the black sky transitioned to midnight blue and gradually grew lighter. A storm cloud with pleasant lightning in the distance off to our left added to the beauty of the setting. Moments later, a thick band of scarlet orange began to form at the horizon, revealing the powerful sun.

As the sunlight shone through, we all burst into tears with pure relief and happiness. We weren't at the top yet, but it sure felt like it in my mind. That light was absolutely crucial for keeping our spirits up and enabling us to move forward. Finally it felt like the progress we had made was real. For the first time in hours we heard laughter and joy running along the mountainside from the excitement of our large group.

The sky continued to slowly wake up, flaunting its natural beauty. It was the most well-earned and beautiful sunrise any of us had ever seen. At that altitude, we were in a position to see it all happen so gradually and on such a large scale. We looked in front of us and saw shades of orange, red, and pink, then turned around and saw the dark, threatening sky we had hiked beneath all night. Now we were just minutes away from reaching the ultimate peak.

Walking through the snow and feeling the resistance of the powder underneath our feet, each step felt difficult, even though the incline wasn't severe. At first we saw it in the distance, wrapping around the crest of a massive crater, our eyes fixated on a collection of signage that read, "Congratulations." At this moment, it is easy to fall into the trap of tunnel vision. After all, you are moments from true success. But we encourage any climber, at this time, to take in their surroundings, as this was surely the most beautiful sight any of us had seen in our entire lives.

As we approached Uhuru Peak, to the left we saw a wall of ice just below. These are the remnants of the glacier, the last remaining glacial formation of the ice cap that once crowned Mt. Kilimanjaro. To the right, we saw the desolate abyss of the Reusch Crater. Behind us, 70 kilometers west of Mt. Kilimanjaro, we saw the silhouette of Mt. Meru, a 14,977-foot summit that was dwarfed by our ascending perspective. We were touching the sky, confronted by the beauty of nature at every angle. The time one can remain at this altitude is limited, and these moments of beauty are fleeting.

Carson arrived at the summit a few minutes ahead of the next nearest climber in our group. Accompanied by his guide, Attley Wales, he reached the Uhuru—which translates to "Freedom"—Peak right at sunrise. He recalled a special moment when they arrived. When he and his guide reached the summit, they were fortunate to have the location to themselves; no other climbing party was there. It was just the two of them and the mountain. A few feet from the congratulatory sign, Attley fell to his knees and raised his hands, embracing the sky. He prayed, not to any specific religious deity, but to the mountain, thanking Kilimanjaro for the safe passage of our group and his colleagues. In this moment of intense spirituality, surrounded by beauty beyond comprehension, Carson couldn't help but be overwhelmed with emotion and filled with gratitude, wonder, and a sense of accomplishment.

For 10 to 20 minutes after arriving at Uhuru Peak, climbers have the opportunity to take photos, congratulate each other, and celebrate the collective effort of all who reach the summit. Plenty of hugs, high fives, and tears of joy are shared. This is a special moment that cannot be fully captured in a photo or by any other medium—the emotion, joy, and pride are far too great. Our recommendation is to be as present and aware of yourself and your peers as possible. Absorb the experience. Make note of how you feel, what you see, what you say. You will likely never have this moment again, and this is what makes it so special. Even though the 21 of us all arrived at Uhuru Peak, some of us knew that we had already summited our own emotional fight, overcoming the mental battle we had all confronted.

Chapter 11

Accidents and Incidents

Bailey Honig

"Yeah, I've broken a bone in my hand before, but I've never had a serious injury," I said to Daniela as we hiked through the rainforest of Mt. Kilimanjaro. It was true: I'd never experienced an injury or even an illness that had greatly affected my ability to perform day-to-day activities. However, that was all about to change.

We arrived at Barafu Camp around mid-afternoon, and all that was on our minds was the seven-hour summit we would face that night starting at midnight. We were now approaching the end of Day Four and I was sick of having to pee every 30–45 minutes from the Diamox we were taking to combat the altitude. Since I knew we would no longer need the Diamox after we reached the peak, I was more than ready to take my last Diamox and never touch those pills again. I took my final Diamox at 5 p.m. and didn't even think about packing another pill for our hike that night.

At the time, I knew good and well that these pills last for up to 12 hours. I also knew that we would be hiking for more than 12 hours after I had taken my last Diamox. If I had thought realistically about the challenge that lay ahead of me that night, I would have sucked it up and brought one more Diamox with me to take during the second half of our climb to the summit. I just couldn't wait to be done with all the annoying side effects of the drug I had lived on for the past few days. Instead, I decided to roll the dice and hope we would make it to the top before my final Diamox wore off. That was my first mistake.

I never expected any part of summiting Mt. Kilimanjaro to be easy, but our seven-hour hike from Barafu Camp was miserable. Climbing through the dark at 18,000-feet altitude was tough, but I have never experienced such a struggle as I did for the last two hours up that mountain. I was struggling for breath after we reached about the halfway point to the peak, and I clearly did not do a great job of hiding that. For the first four or five hours I refused any help and continued to carry my daypack, despite various guides constantly begging me to carry it for the remainder of the night to make my hike easier. Finally, the guides refused to take no for an answer and made me stop and give them my bag. This did wonders for my stamina and made the climb seem much easier, for maybe 20 minutes.

It was around 5 a.m. and I was absolutely drained. I wasn't sure if I was hurting more from the combined 13 hours of hiking that day, a lack of food and water, or the altitude of the highest mountain in Africa. However, I knew for sure that I was exhausted and could not stop rotating between headaches and stomachaches. For over an hour and a half I repeated the same pattern. I would take two or three steps, put my head down, and gasp for breath. Then I would take two or three more steps and continue that pattern. My body refused to let me move any faster, but my adrenaline was at an all-time high. I would have died before I let myself fail to reach the summit that night.

We had made it past Stella Point, our first small victory on the way to the highest point of the mountain, and we were walking through the snow-covered part of Mt. Kilimanjaro. Our final destination was Uhuru Peak. Eventually, one of the guides had seen enough of my pathetic efforts at hiking this freak of a mountain. The guide took my poles out of my hands, locked arms with me, and ran me up to the very top. We were sprinting past the entire group and other hikers, as this guide was determined to get me to the top before my entire body gave out on me.

After 15 minutes of running past various groups of people

through the sleet and snow, we finally made it to Uhuru Peak. It was stunning, and I enjoyed the accomplishment of hiking Africa's highest mountain just as much as I enjoyed the chance to sit down for a grand total of 15 minutes and catch my breath. I wished I could have sat there for an hour, but we had a long day ahead of us and needed to make our way back to Barafu Camp soon.

I knew the beginning of our trek down would be just as hard as the trek up had been, but in a different way. However, I kept telling myself that as we got further down, my altitude sickness would surely get better. The first 20 minutes were tough, but once we left the snowy mountaintop and made our way into the drier, more desert-like part of the mountain, my body began to feel more comfortable with its surroundings. I could finally go for almost 30 minutes at a time without stopping to catch my breath. However, the combination of a steep decline and the sandy ground made hiking down this part of the mountain a challenge of its own. I was taking my time without thinking about how much faster any of my friends were making their way down than I was.

Soon I was at a point where I was keeping a good pace with some of my friends. We all noted how dangerous the terrain was, and we were moving at a comfortable pace. Although I felt fine, one of the guides soon caught up with us and began talking to me.

"I saw you were very sick on the way up," the guide said to me. "Let me help you down."

I politely declined, but the guide was set on giving me a helping hand and getting me down the mountain as fast as possible. After several failed efforts to decline his offer of help, I no longer had the energy to keep turning him down and finally allowed the guide to assist me down the mountain. He took my arm and, just like the last 15 minutes up the mountain, began sprinting full speed down the hill. It felt like we were skiing, the way we were gliding down the mountain, even though it was anything but effortless. I felt like I was going to throw up, as if I were on a high-speed roller coaster and had just eaten a full lunch. It was horrifying.

For the first 20 minutes, I had no energy to fight with this guide. I simply let him run me downhill and prayed that we would soon stop to take a break. Eventually, I had had enough. I was uncomfortable moving at such a fast speed down such a steep slope and genuinely feared for my life. I expressed my discomfort to my guide and told him I needed to stop and sit down for a moment. He pointed me to a rock directly ahead of us where we could sit down.

"Actually, that's a better rock. Let's go over there," the guide said as he pointed to another rock across the trail from us. We had finally begun slowing down, but he decided to give us one last sprint to this rock where I could finally relax—or so I thought.

Just a few steps away from our landing spot, my guide was still sprinting. I was scared we would not have enough time to slow down and would potentially slide into the rock, so I pivoted my foot in an attempt to slow us down (bad idea). As I turned my foot, I tweaked my ankle and fell right out of my guide's reach.

If only that had been the worst of it. Once I fell, my guide also lost his balance, and his entire body weight came crashing onto my right ankle. I heard a very audible "pop." That was the only sound I could hear at that time: the snapping of my ankle bone. It was as if my guide fell on a large bag of air, the way my bone broke.

"OH MY GOD! MY ANKLE! OH MY GOD!" I screamed.

My guide would continue to hear that refrain for the next five minutes, as I knew my body should never have made that noise. My whole right boot immediately expanded as my ankle began to swell. I lay down and could not do anything but breathe and lie there in pain.

My guide was clearly stressed about the situation as well and repeatedly told me to relax. (Because, at an altitude of 18,000 feet with a demolished ankle, why would I not be relaxed?) He immediately went into problem-solving mode and stretched me out. It felt good to lie down and not move my injured leg. However, my guide may have misjudged my injury. He grabbed my ankle and aggressively twisted it three times. POP. POP. POP. He managed to break my ankle bone even further, after breaking it initially with his body weight.

"THAT'S NOT WORKING! STOP! PLEASE STOP!" I screamed.

I could not get this man away from my foot fast enough. My foot felt as if it were in a volcano. It burned with heat as all of the blood rushed toward it while the swelling continued to increase. I was thankful I had made it to the peak, but my mind went numb at the thought of having one good foot to get me through an 18,000-foot hike down.

Eventually, a group of my friends and other guides approached as they saw me rolling on the ground in pain. Some of them asked me if I wanted my boot to come off, but I refused to see what my ankle looked like. My boot had expanded on both sides of my foot, and that was all I needed to know. Realistically, I should have taken the boot off and let the injury run its course.

We sat there for probably 30 minutes debating different ways to get me back to the base camp. There are helicopter landing pads on various parts of the mountain meant for people in critical situations who need to be taken by helicopter to the nearest hospital. Unfortunately for me, there was no landing pad anywhere near where I went down.

Eventually, I hung both my arms around my friends' shoulders as they walked with me down the mountain. At times I lay across four different people's arms as they walked in unison and carried me down. I even got on another guide's shoulders as he walked down the mountain. All of these options were good for 5–10 feet, but it took too much effort to do this for another hour and a half back to the base camp. Eventually, a guide had me ride on his back piggyback style, which turned out to be our best option. I was at a comfortable height and this was the most physically bearable mode for transporting me back to the base camp.

We began hiking into very rocky and narrow terrain. This guide had finally earned my trust, and I let my guard down as we moved into this slippery territory. As my guide took a step up a rock, his body collapsed. I fell off his back and he fell back onto my already broken ankle. I let out a scream and refused to move.

Thankfully for me, a group of five guides came running from ahead of us with a long metal sheet. This would be my stretcher, where I would lie as they carried me back to Barafu Camp. There were thin straps to secure me and no cushions to soften the ride, just a bare metal sheet on which I would lie for whatever time it took the guides to get me back to base camp. I held on to the sides of this makeshift stretcher for an hour and a half as I slid around what felt like my deathbed. I looked out multiple times to see that we were right next to a huge cliff with a steep drop-off.

This is it. This is how I'm going to die, I repeatedly thought to myself. My morale was low, and all I could think of was how in the world I was going to make it down this mountain. At some points, the guides had to take large steps to move down the rocky terrain. When this happened, they had to lift my stretcher up to be almost directly vertical. My head was high up in the air, and all I could hope for was that all five of them could keep their balance and hold me.

After an hour and a half that felt like an eternity, we finally made it back to Barafu Camp.

I lay there as my friends gave me food and their frozen water bladders, which were the closest thing we had to ice packs. I removed my boot and sock, and my ankle was swollen on both sides to the size of a baseball. It still had its color, but it was ugly to look at. Luckily, one of my friends had brought an ACE wrap and wrapped my ankle to aid with the swelling.

After some time, I brought a makeshift ice pack to my tent and caught up on some sleep. However, everyone soon had to leave, as we had a few more hours of hiking down to the next base camp. One of my friends helped me out of my tent to get some lunch, then held me on his shoulder as he carried me to another tent. He had me try to walk on my own, but I could not put any weight on my ankle. A group of guides saw me struggling to walk and insisted that I needed to get to a hospital as soon as possible. Soon, another stretcher arrived with a group of six men who were determined to get me to the bottom of the mountain that day.

Compared to the metal sheet I had lain on earlier, this stretcher felt like a Tempur-Pedic mattress. The guides put a cushion behind my head and fastened two straps around my waist and stomach so I would not slide out of the stretcher. One guide held it from behind, acting as a steerer, one guide carried it in front to keep the pace, and four guides carried the sides.

I didn't know what the future held for me that day, and all I could hope for was that I would make it to the bottom of the mountain. I was too tired to worry about how that would happen. My fate was in the hands of my guides now. I was so tired that within 15 minutes of beginning our descent, I fell asleep. For about an hour, I relaxed on my stretcher as the six guides began a wild run down Mt. Kilimanjaro.

We were taking one of several emergency routes, which are traveled only by people with physical or medical limitations who could not get down the mountain any other way. Eventually I woke up to panting and screaming, as the tired guides grew frustrated. I was dying to know what they were yelling about, but unfortunately I didn't know enough Swahili to understand even a hint of what they were saying. They had stopped to take a breather, so I was just lying on the ground wrapped in my sleeping bag, tied to the stretcher, and still in immense pain. Eventually, the guides started back up again.

I lay there for five straight hours while six people carried me down the mountain. There were times when the path we were traveling became so narrow that the guides on the sides of my stretcher would have to let go. For example, a tree on the path would block a guide's way, so he would have to let go of the stretcher, pivot around the tree, then pick up his side of the stretcher and carry on until he was forced to do the same thing again.

At times one or the other of the guides would slip and fall while they were carrying the stretcher. Sometimes, they tripped over a shoelace that had come undone. Other times, a pebble threw off their balance or a boulder got in their way and sent them flying. In the meantime, although I couldn't see this at the time, Kristin, one of our instructors, was running down the trail to catch up with me so she could accompany me to the hospital.

This trek down was a dirty, sweaty mess. I couldn't believe the guides' stamina and determination as we traveled through all the different ecosystems of the mountain. At some points, I even forgot that my ankle hurt as I just tried to take in the beautiful environments through which I was being run. I was in pain, but hey—you don't get these views in North Carolina.

We were finally approaching what would turn out to be the last hour of our emergency evacuation. All the guides were sweating profusely and panting as we approached hour five of our journey down the mountain. They had grown used to dodging the various trees and stumps that obstructed their path while carrying me down the mountain. Children even started to appear, running up and down the sides of our path, having races with their friends.

Finally we approached an open space within Mt. Kilimanjaro's rainforest that offered a gazebo and a bench where we could rest. Within one day, I had traveled from Uhuru Peak to the bottom of Mt. Kilimanjaro. Here I waited for a van to pick me up and drive me back to our hotel.

From there it took a little over an hour to drive back to our hotel, where I talked to Rob, the director of the company through which we had hired the guides for our trek. Rob contacted a local doctor, who left his house to come and examine the severity of my injury. As I waited for the doctor to arrive, I sat with Kristin, who had run down the mountain with us all day. I stuffed myself with the hotel's pizza as I waited for a man with a doctor's coat to come and examine me.

After about 30 minutes, a man in a blue T-shirt, jeans, and flip flops approached me. I figured he was a friendly stranger and just wanted to make conversation with me.

"What's up, bro? Let me see your ankle."

Who the hell is this guy? I thought to myself. At first I just laughed it off as if he were making a joke. Then I realized that this man who just called me "bro" was my doctor. Oh god.

After telling my newfound friend and doctor the story of how my ankle swelled up to the size of a baseball, he removed my ankle wrap from earlier that day at the base camp. Surprisingly, there was no bruising yet. He then told me that I had either a dislocated ankle or a fracture, and I needed to go to the local hospital in the morning for X-rays. He rubbed some mystery ointment on my ankle for pain, gave me a prescription drug similar to Ibuprofen, re-wrapped my ankle, and that was all for the night.

The next morning, I woke up and unwrapped my ankle so I could wash off in the shower. Not only was my ankle just as swollen, but now it was completely dark blue from bruising. Not a good sign.

Eventually, I left for the hospital. I was expecting a large building with enough rooms to make me feel as lost as I would in a hospital in the US. But this was much different. It felt like I was in a retirement home, the way this hospital was set up. The area where I waited for my X-ray results was completely outside. I looked out into the garden area in front of me as three cats played together under the bushes.

After about half an hour of waiting for my results, the doctors came back with my X-rays. My fibula was broken, which was what my flip-flop-wearing doctor from the night before had suggested. Now I was to be put into a cast at the hospital until I could seek a second opinion back home. The doctor who was to put me in my cast had a few patients to treat ahead of me, so I once again waited in the garden area. After a few patients had come and gone, one of the guides who had brought me to the hospital came up to me.

"We have to wait just a little longer. Your doctor is out at the pharmacy right now to buy supplies to make your cast."

I was shocked that any hospital did not have the inventory to make a cast. However, this apparently was not an uncommon occurrence. This was just another difference I found between hospitals in the US and Tanzania. Soon enough, I received my cast, and I was on my way out. Mt. Kilimanjaro left me with a broken ankle, but also with one hell of a story.

Chapter 12

Day Five: Uhuru Peak to Mweka Camp

Timothy Boles

We made it to the top of Kilimanjaro. It still feels surreal to say. Our group conquered five climate zones, severe altitude sickness, and serious stomach issues that we hope never to experience again. Even though it felt a little silly to take them at the time, I'm thankful we took pictures at the Uhuru Peak, because those were inevitably shared with everyone we had ever met.

After summiting the mountain, inevitably, you must begin the descent. As you are climbing, you have the goal of reaching the peak to motivate you to keep moving up the mountain. Going down, the only thought that I and many others had was, *Oh my god, I cannot believe I just did that. Now get me the hell off this damn mountain.*

Even though the ascent was challenging, the descent posed its own struggles. Your journey down the mountain, if it's anything like ours, can best be described by a line from Beyoncé's hit song "Halo": "Baby, we're tumbling down." This chapter will relate our experiences making our way down the mountain. Hopefully, our experience can offer lessons that will help future climbers prepare physically and mentally for the journey down. And if not, those future climbers may at least get a few laughs.

Up to Day Five, we devoted our time and energy to working tirelessly to reach the top of what seemed like an endless mountain. Once we left the Uhuru Peak sign and turned back toward Stella Point, our journey back down began. The return trip to Stella Point was not that difficult, with a relatively straight path and a gentle but steady decline. What made this portion of the hike difficult was the fact that we were at an altitude of 19,000 feet, where the oxygen was thin and even forming a coherent thought could be extremely difficult. Additionally, we were battling the inevitable exhaustion that resulted from having just hiked for seven hours through the night. We thought cramming for a test and pulling an all-nighter was difficult, but this challenge was unmatched.

At this point in the hike, we were in what is considered the "arctic zone," a climate characterized by an icy and rocky terrain with no plant or animal life. At one point, I dropped my water bottle, and because of the ice, it rapidly slid down the side of the mountain—an action that I noted was not LNT (Leave No Trace) approved. As we made our way back to Stella Point, our only thought was to keep putting one foot in front of the other, being intentional about where we stepped so we would not end up like my water bottle, rocketing down into the abyss of the mountain. We stuck to the path, making sure to step in the footprints of the porter we were following.

After hiking for what felt like three hours but was in reality about 45 minutes, our group made it to Stella Point, where we were given a five-minute break for water and to acknowledge the fact that we had made it to the top of Mt. Kilimanjaro. None of us realized how grateful we would be for that short break, because nothing could have prepared us for the next part of our downhill journey, when the sun was starting to rise and the once-hard rock we had climbed up earlier began to turn into an almost sand-like consistency.

From Stella Point at 18,885 feet we hiked a different path to descend to Barafu Camp at 15,239 feet. The decline during this part of the hike was much steeper than we expected. The main mission for our guides and for us on this leg of the hike was to reach a lower altitude as fast as possible. And when I say as fast as possible, I mean as fast as possible. In talking with other students from the course, many reported feeling that they had been rushed down the mountain by the porters. The reason for this "rushing" is that the porters are trying to get you to a place where you actually remember what it feels like to take a deep breath—which is understandable, but was still very stressful in the moment.

The path from Stella Point down to Barafu Camp consists primarily of a series of switchbacks made of loose pebbles, a challenge many members of our group were unprepared for. To envision what it's like to navigate this terrain, imagine alpine skiing down a black diamond hill. As soon as we started down this path, we realized this was going to be a completely hellish experience.

We progressed down the path, slowly putting one foot in front of the other. I relied heavily on my hiking poles to avoid completely falling down, which was mostly successful. We repeated this process for maybe 15 minutes, though it felt more like four hours. Most of the other members of our group were passing me; thankfully, one of the porters noticed I was struggling and helped me by taking my bag, which was a touching act of kindness.

The relief of no longer carrying my bag made me feel like a new person; I hadn't realized what a difference it would make. It was easier for me not only to breathe but also to maintain my balance, and I no longer had to rest after every step. For all of us, giving up our packs and handing them to a guide was a humbling act, but it was also a great metaphor for life, reminding us that it is okay to struggle sometimes and asking for help is an act of strength. This was one of the lessons we took with us from the mountain.

We continued to descend and our group began to thin out, spreading out with various guides based on our speed and comfort level with the decline. Some hikers moved slowly and steadily down the mountain, while others were rushed down the mountain with the help of the guides. Those led by the guides looked like they were sprinting all the way to the bottom, as though they were in a sled. After hiking for an hour and a half and negotiating countless switchbacks, it felt like the end was finally in sight. We had made it down the slippery slope of rocks, and now all that was left was an hour and a half of relatively uneventful hiking—or so we thought.

When we reached the end of the sliding mountain of rocks, a few of us clumped together to make it more of a group descent again. One of the students in the group, Bailey, had broken his ankle on the hike down and was unable to walk. Eventually, other students caught up to us, and together we tried to develop a plan to get Bailey back to Barafu Camp.

Thankfully the group included a biology student who was hoping to go to medical school and another student who was trained in wilderness first aid. Together, they were the closest thing we had to a medical professional. We tried a series of different splints and techniques to help transport Bailey. Unfortunately, everything we tried fell apart, and the limited oxygen made it difficult for us to move him more than five steps without being completely out of breath. In the span of an hour, we had moved a few hundred feet and we were all exhausted and dehydrated.

This continued for about another 30 minutes until in the distance we saw six men rounding the corner with a stretcher. At that moment, I fell to the ground and nearly cried tears of joy. We had never been more relieved and excited to see anyone in our whole lives.

After the stretcher arrived, the rest of our journey to Barafu Camp was rather uneventful. The path was much easier than the mountain of sliding rocks we had just endured. We hiked for another hour until finally, in the distance, we saw our familiar yellow North Face tents. As soon as we saw the tents, you could feel the spirits of our group begin to rise and our pace quicken. All any of us wanted was to lie down and sleep, even if it would only be a quick nap before we resumed hiking.

When we finally made it back to camp, we made a beeline toward our tents. In the tents, most of us stripped off all the cold-weather clothes we had now entirely sweated through and lay down on top of our sleeping bags, where we each had the best nap of our lives, both exhausted and happy. We were allowed to sleep for two hours before being awoken by the face of a friendly porter knocking on our tent, saying we needed to start packing to get ready to hike to Mweka Camp.

We grudgingly began to pack up our belongings. Even though we had descended in altitude significantly, we still had little oxygen going to our brains, and we each had a general desire not to hike for six more hours. This meant we moved slowly, taking 45 minutes to pack up our limited number of items. After a few cups of hot tea and a pep talk from our professors and the more energetic members of the group, we were ready to start the six-hour hike from Barafu Camp to Mweka Camp.

Given that we had already been hiking for upwards of 10 hours that day, it is safe to say that our motivation was extremely low. The best part of this portion of the hike was that with each step we took, we could almost feel our lungs getting more and more oxygen. We hadn't realized how much the altitude impacted us until it was no longer a variable. It was on this leg of the hike that we were able to have conversations while walking again, which made the time pass much quicker.

The terrain down to Mweka Camp was a rocky road, literally, as if someone had added a giant set of rock stairs to the side of the mountain. This quickly began to take a toll on us physically, so we decided to treat ourselves with frequent 15- to 20-minute snack breaks. These breaks were crucial for our physical strength and emotional motivation. Even though some members of the group walked more quickly than others, each cluster of people was cracking jokes the whole time and getting to know the guides better. Every time we sat down for a snack break, our porter, Dennis, would roll his eyes and say we needed to keep moving in order to reach the camp before dark, but in an empathetic tone that told us he knew how hard this day was for us. Eventually, after many aching steps and countless snack breaks, we made it to Mweka Camp—proud of ourselves for persevering through the hardship and even choosing a slightly further campsite, to make the final day of hiking as easy as it could be.

Chapter 13

Day Six: Mweka Camp to Mweka Base

Meg Rude

Tell the story of the mountain you climbed. Your words could become a page in someone else's survival guide.
Morgan Harper Nichols

When we woke up after our last night on the mountain, we were ready to use whatever energy we had left to get off the mountain. At breakfast, everyone was thinking about being back in civilization. We took in our surroundings, and as we looked up we could see the peak of Kilimanjaro, which was almost always covered in clouds. It was surreal to think about how far we had come, and we all felt immensely proud.

As a group, we had the chance to thank the porters, guides, and cooks and present them with the soccer ball we had brought along as a gift. We took group pictures and sang together one last time. By now most of us had learned the lyrics to the songs they had sung to us, so we all joined in, singing together in a big circle. It was genuinely sad to say goodbye to them, as they were such a significant part of our journey.

We had been told the last leg of our journey would take about three hours, which some of our class members decided in retrospect was a bald-faced lie. Our "three-hour" hike through the jungle took place on a trail that was basically a mudslide. Given that we had all fallen a few times the previous day, our approach on this final day was to take our time and be careful. We started the last leg of the journey together and slowly broke off into groups going various paces, some wanting to jog down the mountain, willing to risk a few rolled ankles, and others wanting to savor those last moments together on the hike.

The hike that day felt unending. That could have been due to the fact that we were sore, ready to be off the mountain, and taking our sweet time so as not to fall. One group described their final walk as individual, with some people listening to music while others took the opportunity to walk in silence and reflect on the overall hike. Other people chatted with their guides and tried to learn as much as they could about the guides' lives and experiences in Tanzania and their work for the trekking company. We split up a little depending on the type of hike we wanted, which made everyone's journey down the mountain a little more special.

As the youngest member of the group, Meg used this time to reflect on the entire journey. She had gone on this trip to push herself beyond her comfort level and get outside her regular routine. She was not normally a hiker and had never actually camped before. Although she exercised occasionally, preparing for this trip physically and mentally was completely foreign to her.

Like many other members of our group, Meg came to the conclusion that she should have done more research about Mt. Kilimanjaro prior to the trip. But we also all decided that it could have been our naiveté that pushed us into this adventure without a second thought. Each day on the mountain was a small shock for most of us.

During this walk, which was almost completely downhill and physically less exhausting, we had time to reflect on the numerous occasions when we had asked ourselves, "Why did I sign up for this?" But after being quite literally on the other side of the mountain, it felt much more worth it. The hike was no longer an uphill, anxiety-inducing march to the top. Instead, we walked with confidence, knowing the hardest part was behind us—and a few thousand feet above us. Our recognition that these memories and experiences would last a lifetime and the lessons we learned would sink deep into our personalities made the difficulty seem much less significant in retrospect.

At this point in the hike we were fully in the jungle, and we started to see various kinds of monkeys swinging in the trees around us. Sadly, that wasn't a sign that we were near the gate. Once we reached the dirt road, however, we were nearly there. During this final hour of the hike, Tim and Katherine, who had become close friends during the trip, stopped to make a pact. They jokingly agreed that when their bodies start to hurt on a regular basis as much as they did at this moment, probably around the age of 40, they would go paragliding and let go, in order to avoid ever feeling this much pain again. The pain was a warning that with less than an hour left of walking, our bodies had nearly reached their breaking point.

When we finally saw the Mweka gate in the distance, we thought we were hallucinating. Even though it was a long time coming, it seemed very strange to think that our entire hike was finished. There was a sign that said "Congratulations! Bon Voyage!" that everyone stopped to take pictures around. There was Wi-Fi at the gate, so we all took out our phones—which had been useless on the trail—and let our parents know that we were alive and had made it to the top.

For many of us, being completely off the grid for six days was truly meaningful. We were able to soak in the entire experience, only using our phones to take pictures when it felt appropriate. It felt so strange to take my phone off airplane mode and communicate with the world again. There was something about living in the present and not feeling tied to a device that made the whole experience even more powerful.

After everyone had reached the gate and communicated with their parents, it was time to start the bus ride back to our hotel in Moshi. We stopped at a restaurant for lunch and I can say without a doubt that a Coke and a Kilimanjaro Beer had never hit the spot as much as they did at that moment. We all agreed they were definitely better than mountain water.

There was a gift shop attached to the restaurant, which gave us the perfect time to get our souvenir shopping done. Even though it felt a little touristy and detracted from the authenticity of the moment, we knew our friends and family members would be disappointed if we didn't come home with some physical display of our time on the mountain and in Tanzania. From the lunch spot it was about a 30-minute bus ride back to the hotel. Being back in civilization was definitely a strange feeling after being on the mountain for six days.

Once back at the hotel everyone rushed to their rooms to shower. And by "rushed," I mean we slowly and painfully limped toward our rooms, because the soreness had really begun to set in, especially for those of us whose rooms were on the second floor. At this point our bodies were mush, but the hot shower felt amazing on our joints. The water pooled to brown at our feet, washing away the accumulated dirt.

We looked in the mirror after being freshly showered and noted, even without verifying it on the scale, that we had all lost about 10 pounds. We all looked significantly thinner in our faces and the men especially seemed to have dropped a lot of the fat and muscle they had when they started the trip. Some of the women noticed their jeans were much looser, although we lost the most weight in our chests, some of us dropping a few cup sizes, which became noticeable on our trip to a swimming hole the following day.

In the days that followed the hike, we reflected on how we all had survived shitting our pants, terrible headaches, loss of appetite, puking our guts out, and struggling to breathe when we needed air the most. Before we posted the Instagram pictures or even celebrated with each other, we each took a moment to be immensely proud of ourselves. We were among the 35,000 people who attempted to summit Kilimanjaro yearly, which made us both incredibly lucky to have the opportunity and also part of a greater community of hikers.

When we all met back in the lobby, it was time to celebrate. We each received a certificate for hiking Mt. Kilimanjaro along with some Trekking Hero swag. Then we went to Peppers Bar in Moshi for a much-deserved feast. When the pizza and curry landed family-style on the table, we ate it voraciously and rapidly while laughing and talking with a few of our guides. That night we all slept well in our beds, prepared to be the sorest we had ever been the next morning. For each of us, reflecting on the trip had barely begun, as we each approached in our own way and time the process of making meaning of this incredible experience.

Chapter 14

Leave No Trace

Megan Barber and Morgan Collins

Huddled in the blue dining tent on our last evening on the mountain, we reminisced about the trials and tribulations of our journey up and down Kilimanjaro. Naturally, the conversation turned to bathroom issues. Our loveable ginger, Jack DiPietro, admitted to having to throw a pair of boxers down *the hole*, too ruined to salvage. "I have to say, I left a fucking trace," Jack admitted to everyone.

The class roared at Jack's comment. The "Leave No Trace" (LNT) lingo had been somewhat of a joke, inevitably intertwined with the concept of carrying around one's own used toilet paper for six days. Levity helps in such a situation. But the principles behind Leave No Trace, which were developed by the Leave No Trace Center for Outdoor Ethics in Boulder, Colorado, are no laughing matter. The number of climbers on Kilimanjaro has increased dramatically since the first hiking route was created in 1965, and so, too, has the human impact.

As people who love exploring the outdoors, we believe natural spaces are worth protecting, especially in a world in which environmental landscapes are dwindling. Although our group possessed a range of experiences with the outdoors, we all agreed that there was something special about Mt. Kilimanjaro. From being immersed in the endless shades of green in the rainforest to being surrounded by clouds in the alpine desert, our relationship with nature changed while hiking. Never before had we been so in tune with the intricate balance of ecosystems, and our thoughts often turned to how we were impacting the land as we hiked.

Carrying around a bag of your own toilet paper and personal trash is no pleasant task, but this chapter will offer readers some tips to make it easier to protect the environment we all came to love and to have as little environmental impact as possible. Climbing Kilimanjaro is unquestionably a privilege, and we realized that the best way to thank the mountain for the time we spent there was to make it seem as though we had never been there at all: to leave no trace.

The Importance of "Leave No Trace"

The goal of LNT, both as an organization and as a set of practices, is to raise awareness of the impact humans can have on the natural environment, while also educating the population about ways to minimize their impact when they do choose to enjoy the great outdoors. The goal of both the organization and the practices is to leave things the way we found them, to be mindful of others (both human and otherwise), and to *appreciate* nature. The human impact on nature is evident almost everywhere—from litter and pollution to damaged trails and endangered wildlife, and everything in between. However, this impact is not inevitable. Most of these problems can easily be avoided; the issues are mainly caused by misinformation and, at times, indifference. The principles of LNT ensure that we can enjoy time spent in nature without damaging or disrupting the natural world. After this course we realized more than ever that it is our job to protect Mother Earth.

Although Leave No Trace was originally designed for backcountry settings, its principles have been adapted to apply anywhere, from remote wilderness areas to local parks to our own backyards. Seven general principles comprise LNT; however, the principles are constantly evolving to produce the best possible results when put into practice. The LNT Center for Outdoor Ethics regularly examines, evaluates, and revises the principles to ensure that they are up to date with the latest research and findings from biologists, land managers, and various leaders in outdoor education.

How to *Not* "Leave a Fucking Trace"

The Leave No Trace ideology incorporates the following seven principles:

1. Plan and prepare
2. Travel and camp on durable surfaces
3. Dispose of waste properly
4. Leave what you find
5. Minimize campfire impacts
6. Respect wildlife
7. Be considerate of other visitors

To achieve our goal of not leaving a trace on Kilimanjaro, we devised our own principles based on this ideology:

1. *Prepare for the hole.* The hole, or the bathrooms at the camps that are quite aptly named, are somewhere you want to spend as little time as possible. Here are some ways you can make that happen and still minimize your ecological footprint.

    a. *Use wilderness wipes.* If you use biodegradable wilderness wipes instead of toilet paper, you can leave your wipes in the hole and not have to worry about carrying them around with you. If you choose to use them while on the trail, make sure they are not visible to the human eye in any way when you discard them. Although it might be a little gross to carry the wipes, taking them with you is always the best way to minimize your own impact.

    b. *Take hand sanitizer.* You're going to want to wash your hands as soon as you leave the hole, so just take it with you when you go.

c. *The shit bag.* If you don't bring biodegradable wipes or toilet paper, you're going to want to designate a bag for the "used" products. This is a Ziploc bag that you cover in duct tape; this way the contents can't be seen or smelled as you carry it along the trail. Ladies, you're gonna want to bring one no matter what. The altitude can do strange things to a menstrual cycle, and we can attest to this.

2. *Follow the guides.* You won't have to worry about figuring out where to camp or where to walk because your amazing guides will be with you the whole way. Just follow them!

a. *Follow in the guides' footsteps. Literally.* When on the trail, it was so helpful to watch where the guides walked to figure out where the ground was solid enough to step on to avoid causing soil or rocks to shift. Even though it might be tempting to wander off the beaten path, that will only create new paths that will be destructive to the landscape.

b. *Camp at the designated campsite.* When you arrive at the campsite each night, the porters will already have set up your tents for you. You should certainly explore the campsite and its surroundings, especially at Shira Camp where you can go into a cave. But to minimize your impact, you should stay relatively close to the campsite and sleep only at the designated campsite.

c. *Don't stray too far off the trail.* Thanks to Diamox and the endless liters of water you're drinking, you will have to take constant pee breaks. When you do, try to find an area where you will not disturb the vegetation (e.g., behind a rock, or on a small animal trail) to minimize your impact on the local ecosystems.

3. *Don't be trashy.* Whatever waste you create while climbing, from snack wrappers to toilet paper, needs to be carried off the mountain with you. No exceptions.

   a. *Carry all your trash the whole way.* Sadly, there was already noticeable litter along the trail. This doesn't make littering acceptable—make sure you take all your trash with you. You can also pick up the trash that others have left behind; you can even use your hiking poles to do this. It's a nice gesture to the people who will be hiking Kilimanjaro after you leave.

   b. *Cover your trash bag in duct tape so you don't have to look at it.* A bag of trash becomes pretty gross after six days. If you cover it in opaque duct tape, you—and everyone else—won't have to see whatever waste you may have collected along the way.

   c. *Try to bring snacks that produce as little trash as possible.* Rather than bringing individually wrapped snacks, try to bring snacks in single packages, such as large bags of trail mix. These larger snacks can always be put into a smaller reusable container for each day. This decreases the possibility of leaving a wrapper behind every time you take a break for a snack on the trail, which becomes very easy to do when you are moving quickly.

4. *Don't steal a giant groundsel.* The Latin name for this plant is *Dendrosenecio kilimanjari* because it *only* grows on Kilimanjaro. This principle is pretty simple: leave things that belong on the mountain *on the mountain*. The principle serves a dual purpose: your bag won't become heavier from all the rocks you never collected, and the ecosystem will be left undisturbed. Pictures are just as good as the real thing.

5. *We didn't start the fire—and neither will you.* Another simple

rule: there are no campfires allowed in Kilimanjaro National Park. As enjoyable as it would have been to have a nice warm fire to sit around on some of the colder nights, trust us, you will grow to love the dining and sleeping tents and how they trap body heat. A hot cup of tea always helps too! You can build a fire and make s'mores on another camping trip, just not on Kilimanjaro.

6. *Don't feed the monkeys.* This rule will be hard to follow and we didn't do a perfect job of this, but don't feed the monkeys. They don't need you and they're better off without you. If you take some time to walk alone through the rainforest, you might be quiet enough to see some of the rarer monkeys in their natural habitats, which was much cooler than seeing them swarm as we ate lunch.

7. *Jambo.* You will pass plenty of other hikers and lots of porters and guides while you are hiking. Be considerate of their experiences, be friendly, and say *Jambo!*

This list is not exhaustive, but it was something we practiced during our hike in the hope that we left the natural world the same as or better than we found it.

Chapter 15

Privilege and Ecotourism

Junie Burke and Katherine Field

How to Assess Your Privilege

Before traveling to Tanzania, it is necessary to understand your own privilege and biases, as you are about to experience a new country with a different culture, language, and way of life. By assessing our own privilege and biases, we prepared ourselves for a learning opportunity and a chance to increase our cultural competence. To value human differences and pursue mutual respect, we first needed to understand privilege so we could address our own blind spots and judgments when entering this new culture.

Social privilege allows individuals with certain identities to have specific experiences depending on whether theirs is a dominant or subordinate identity. Peggy McIntosh defines privilege as occurring when "one group has something of value that is denied to others simply because of the groups they belong to, rather than because of anything they've done or failed to do" (Johnson, 2006). Privilege is a social construction through which particular groups of people are oppressed as a result of characteristics or identities over which they may have no control.

Often, privilege in the US is determined by race, ethnicity, gender, sexual orientation, religion, age, nationality, ability, and/ or social class, among other factors. The dominant identities in the US include White, American-born, heterosexual, Christian-identifying, young, able-bodied, upper-middle class, and male. Individuals with one or more of these dominant identities have access to privilege that is denied to those whose identities place them in the subordinate groups.

The fact that our class was able to travel to Tanzania to hike Mt. Kilimanjaro clearly reveals our economic privilege. Elon University gave us the opportunity to study abroad and have such an impactful trekking experience, but there was a hefty cost associated with it. At our university, there is an extra cost to study abroad; in addition, we had an expensive packing list that was necessary to ensure that we had the proper gear while climbing Mt. Kilimanjaro. These were added expenses on top of the already expensive tuition cost of a prestigious private institution.

Additionally, we paid for guides, porters, and cooks to help us make it up the mountain, carry our belongings, and prepare our meals and campsite every night. While this service benefited the economy of Tanzania and provided jobs for these local workers, it was important for us to examine our intentions for our experience on the mountain, because we wanted to be culturally responsive to and respectful of the porters, guides, and cooks. Before embarking on the Kilimanjaro trek, we reflected on the following principles:

1. Pursue self-awareness on an ongoing basis
2. Ensure respect when interacting with individuals, groups, and communities
3. Value human difference

Reflecting on these three ideas helped us identify how each of us brought our own privilege and power into this new culture.

Pursuing self-awareness on an ongoing basis required constant vigilance regarding how we were coming across to the people of Tanzania, based on our privilege as American ecotourists. It is a valuable exercise to identify the areas in one's life in which privilege either helps or hinders you. Keeping our thoughts, opinions, and biases in mind while experiencing a new culture helped us understand how and why we think about things the way we do.

Additionally, it was important that we were respectful when interacting with everyone in Tanzania. The local population allowed us to enter their world and it was our responsibility to listen intently and respect what they said and did.

Lastly, it was critical to recognize and value the different experiences between the American and Tanzanian cultures. Such awareness lays the groundwork for a successful cultural exchange and learning opportunity, and we wanted to maintain this perspective when we encountered experiences that were different from our American norms.

Privilege in Ecotourism

Awareness of our own privilege and role in Tanzania was powerful, because it allowed us to exercise our privilege in the most beneficial way for the Tanzanian natives. One way to achieve such a beneficial impact is through ecotourism. According to Mtapuri and Giampiccoli (2019), the term *ecotourism* is often misunderstood, and this term and those surrounding it must be properly defined.

Sustainable tourism looks holistically at the economic, cultural, and environmental impact on a community, while community-based tourism focuses on a local level of responsibilities and tourism "development and management" (Dangi & Jamal, 2016). Sustainable community-based tourism partners with locals to help the local economy and culture instead of disrupting it. Mtapuri and Giampiccoli (2019) and Strobl, Teichmann, and Peters (2015) agree that it is difficult to provide a single, clear definition of ecotourism. This causes confusion among tourists and locals alike and allows the term to be marketed by companies or stakeholders while requiring them to make no substantive changes to their actual practices.

To practice "real" ecotourism, tourists traveling to

Tanzania to climb Mt. Kilimanjaro should remain wary of how ecotourism, and tourism in general, is marketed. Although Mtapuri and Giampiccoli (2019) compare a variety of definitions of ecotourism, their article concludes not by providing a single definition of the term, but instead by calling for governments to establish formal definitions of ecotourism to protect it from misuse by those seeking to manipulate the term for economic gain. An example of such an official definition, according to Mtapuri and Giampiccoli (2019), is provided by the State of Queensland government, which defines ecotourism as "ecologically sustainable tourism with a primary focus on experiencing natural areas that fosters environmental and cultural understanding, appreciation and conservation." With such a definition in mind, it is easier to begin assessing privilege in light of ecotourism, without the influence of commercial motivation or gain.

Mt. Kilimanjaro is a popular tourist attraction, and locals are abundantly aware of this. It was clear from our time in Moshi that the locals recognized our tourist status from the way we talked, behaved, and above all, from the way we looked. Our class did not spend much time in Moshi outside of the hotel, except for a dinner at an Indian sports bar on the night we returned from the mountain and a short walk around the block the next day, which consisted largely of locals approaching us with various paintings, bracelets, and other souvenirs to sell.

This experience on the streets of Moshi was uncomfortable for the majority of the class. Reflecting on the experience, students expressed frustration and discomfort. At one point, a man yelled at our group from a car parked next to the sidewalk, "You white! Give me money!" This pretty much sums up the experience. We felt awkward and wished we had not been put in that position, but we also wished the societal circumstances that led to this scenario could have been different.

On our last full day in Tanzania, our class visited Chemka

Hot Springs. We traveled the two-and-a-half hours from the hotel by safari truck, passing through two villages on our way there. We had no idea what the villages were called or where we were, but the drivers of the trucks made sure to pull over to the side of the road to explain the significance of the baobab tree or whatever crop was nearest to us. During some parts of the journey, we saw locals out and about, going about their daily activities. The occupants of one of the trucks, which had paused on the side of the road, were addressed by a local, who reprimanded a student for taking photos. The students in the truck later described their feelings at this moment, which, similar to our short tour of Moshi, included feeling unwelcome, frustratingly misunderstood, and embarrassed while driving through the villages.

These are situations other tourists will likely find themselves encountering on a trip to climb Mt. Kilimanjaro, especially if you plan to spend time in the city of Moshi or the surrounding areas. They are also situations that can be addressed and improved through the study of our own privilege and its relationship to ecotourism before beginning a trip to Tanzania. Before departure, it would have been useful to research how to practice proper ecotourism; that is, how to travel as sustainably as possible and with as much reverence and respect as possible for the local culture.

Depending on the type of travel company a tourist uses to book their trip, the trip may include additional experiences beyond the climb. Our class hadn't conducted any research prior to these experiences, and the responsibility for ecotourism should not be left to whichever company is employed. After researching ecotourism in Tanzania and before departure, it may be helpful to begin a dialogue with the travel company and request to travel in an ecotourist way that does not exploit or exoticize locals or the Tanzanian culture.

On our last morning in Tanzania, hours before our flight back to the US, our class visited a coffee farm outside of Moshi. The people there immediately welcomed us and encouraged us to begin picking coffee beans. They then led us through a coffee-making lesson, which incorporated songs and ended with us drinking the coffee we'd made with our hosts.

As our hosts led us through the process, they noted significant cultural aspects and taught us about Tanzania's unique climate. The experience was warm, welcoming, and informative. Much different from our short tour of Moshi, the coffee tour highlighted cultural differences and awareness. This experience was the best-case scenario and an example of what ethical tourism can look like; we learned about the culture of Tanzania while engaging with locals and feeling welcome. This was ecotourism at work.

Conversations on the Mountain

Katherine, one of the funniest members of our group, did not expect to have such meaningful conversations and interactions with the porters and guides during her trek. On the mountain, there were times when she would find herself walking closely with one of our guides and Katherine had to actively decide whether to engage with them and ask them questions. This experience taught us that we, as global citizens, need to interact with those who have different life experiences to enhance our understanding and respect for human differences. Pushing ourselves to have cross-cultural conversations was one of the most important things we could do while hiking, and in the end those relationships might be even more memorable than the hike itself.

One of Katherine's most meaningful conversations occurred on the descent from the summit. Due to her utter exhaustion, she was walking arm in arm with a guide named Dennis. During their three-hour walk down to Barafu Camp, Katherine and the guide began to share stories of their families, traditions, and lives at home. There is a general belief that international travel provides opportunities to learn about other cultures, but what made this particular conversation so significant were the shared connections they found.

At the same time, this particular conversation was also difficult, as Dennis began sharing his daily struggles to provide for his family. He explained that the Tanzanian government does not offer public education after primary school, so his 12-year-old daughter was not in school because he could not afford it. He explained that if a parent wants their child to continue to receive an education after primary school, they must be able to pay for the school as well as the supplies, clothing, food, and other extra costs. It was deeply saddening to hear Dennis talk about this, as he was disheartened to admit that he could not provide for his daughter in the way he wanted to. Dennis discussed the poverty of Tanzania and how being a guide on Kilimanjaro was seen as one of the better jobs available; yet despite this, he still could not afford education in Tanzania.

The guide was interested in learning about Katherine's life as a college student in the US, as the two educational systems are so different. He was intrigued to learn that Katherine lived with roommates and attended school very far away from her own family and from where she grew up. Sharing that information illuminated for Katherine how much we take education for granted in the US. Additionally, Dennis was amazed to learn that Katherine was a psychology major. He seemed confused upon hearing that mental health was a serious problem in the US and did not know that an entire profession existed to learn more about it.

This conversation struck Katherine in a new way, as she realized some of the systemic differences between the US and Tanzania. Katherine said, "I have always known that my elite, private school education was a huge privilege, but rarely did I think about how this impacts every aspect of my entire life—my future career, the way I think and view the world." Overall, this conversation made us reflect on privilege and how we can process and perceive our own privilege in a whole new light.

From this conversation with Dennis, Katherine realized there are various ways one can think about privilege. Her first emotions in response to this conversation were sadness and anger; it was hard to justify why she is able to afford a private college education while a guide on Kilimanjaro cannot even afford to send his 12-year-old daughter to school. However, she realized that it is not her duty to feel sad or angry. Rather, Katherine learned that it is important to use her privilege to be an activist for those who are oppressed and do not have an equal voice. Feelings of guilt, anger, or sadness about one's own privilege or others' lack of it will not change another person's circumstances. This conversation inspired all of us to continue fighting for social change at the individual, communal, and systemic levels.

Junie, a member of our group who was always smiling, was lucky enough to have meaningful conversations with many of the guides on her way up and down the mountain. On Day Three of the climb, just after lunch, she began walking with a smaller group that had slowly separated from the others. This day was intensely foggy; after about an hour we could no longer see the group ahead of us. The terrain was uphill and difficult that day, and because we had just eaten lunch, Junie began feeling sluggish and her stomach was churning.

One of the guides stopped her and asked how she was feeling, and they embarked on a conversation about his life in Tanzania and his work for the travel company. Junie asked him about the quality of his life and his experiences working for the company. He hesitated at first and finally said he enjoyed the work and the job.

However, later that day, the guide approached her and asked for her email address, which seemed like an ominous request on a mountain with no Wi-Fi. He said he wanted to speak with her more about the travel company, but "not here." Unfortunately, Junie was never able to exchange email addresses with the guide, but the experience nonetheless left her wary of the travel company and should serve as a reminder of the awareness necessary when choosing a travel company in Tanzania. Although we didn't know any better at the time, in retrospect we realized that we should have done more research.

On our second day coming down from the mountain, Junie found herself separated in the middle of the group with a guide. His sleeping mat had detached from his pack repeatedly due to a broken clasp, so they both stopped a few times to readjust it. At one stopping point, several porters trotted by. Junie smiled at them as they quickly ran by, and one of them yelled something at her. The guide looked at Junie and asked, "Do you know what he said?" Junie shook her head. "He said, 'You are very pretty. Marry me.'" This interaction ignited a conversation on catcalling culture in Tanzania, the role of women in society, and, at one point, the guide's relationship with his mother and sisters.

Junie chatted with the guide about the differences between the US and Tanzania, and learned about some of the outdated ideologies that permeate Tanzanian culture. Despite the differences between the two countries, there were also many similarities, as both still had a long way to go in certain social contexts. The guide also asked her about the state of American relations with North Korea, which struck Junie as especially interesting. The US is watched closely by many other countries, yet the average American does not pay close attention to international politics. Such conversations were a blatant reminder of the privilege we exercise when traveling to a country such as Tanzania for the purpose of climbing Mt. Kilimanjaro.

Tanzania is bigger and more complex than just Kilimanjaro,

yet it is up to the tourist to determine the extent to which they want to learn about and engage in the culture they visit. Though asking questions and initiating conversations is privilege in action, tourists can begin to exchange information cross-culturally by sharing stories and experiences that bridge diverse backgrounds and perspectives.

Our Journey Began...

Our journey began in a classroom on the second floor of Alamance Building at Elon University on May 2, 2019. Dr. Rodney Parks tried to prepare the 21 students who had registered for COR 331: Wilderness and Adventure Therapy. "Expect the unexpected," Parks said as his students left the room, eight months out from attempting to summit the tallest freestanding mountain in the world.

Parks has led six groups of Elon students on trips to Peru for the study abroad component of his core capstone course. Taking students hiking on the Inca Trail and through the Rainbow Mountains is no simple task. "Anytime you travel abroad, you risk routine illnesses such as flu and dysentery, but additional challenges that we face in Peru are how students are impacted by the physical components of the class and the impact of altitude. I always tell the students that you have to be comfortable being uncomfortable when it comes to hiking mountains at high altitude," Parks said.

Seemingly undaunted by these risks, Parks moved on to bigger peaks in 2018, when he began planning a class with the goal of summiting Mt. Kilimanjaro, the highest peak in Africa. Measuring in at 19,341 feet, the volcano towers over Tanzania and neighboring Kenya. "Elon students have high levels of resilience and push themselves to make the most of their Elon experience. For the last couple of years I had wondered if we could take a class to do one of the famous Seven Summits, the highest mountains on each of the seven continents. Climbing to the summit of all of them is a mountaineering challenge that many strive to achieve in their lifetime," Parks said.

Parks, who has both a PhD in Counseling and a Master of Social Work, did not miss the opportunity to ask his Wilderness and Adventure Therapy students how they were feeling during that first meeting in May. Students were asked to describe their emotions in one word. The first 10 students used words emphasizing their courage and preparedness, like "eager" or "excited," until one student shared how she really felt: "scared."

"I had never been into camping or hiking. The first time I went camping was over Fall Break, less than four months before leaving for Tanzania. And it was only for one night. So I really didn't know what I was getting myself into," Junie Burke, class of '20, reported. Burke wasn't alone in her fear. As the first Elon class to attempt to summit Kilimanjaro, we were trailblazers. Fear of the unknown plagued me in the months leading up to the climb: What if I went all the way to Tanzania and wasn't able to summit?

Parks decided to scope out the mountain on his own over the summer, to be able to answer students' questions and relieve fears. "I always make sure to visit any site that I intend to take students, to make sure we are well prepared to keep everyone safe on our journey," Parks said.

As Parks embarked on his climb sans students, the class began preparing for hiking by training and collecting gear. Hikers are expected to carry up to 20 pounds (lots of snacks and water) in their day packs, while porters carry all other gear and supplies. Some students practiced hiking with their packs before leaving for Kilimanjaro. "I would take my pack to the gym and fill it with weights and hop on the stair climber and give it a shot. And the feeling of fear really motivated me," Burke said. "There was almost a sense of urgency. I think I ended up being more physically prepared than I needed to be. Working out with other students who were preparing for the class really helped. Even though we were all a little nervous, if we were preparing together, we'd be ready together."

Twenty pounds is heavy, but it is nothing compared

to the nearly 50 pounds of gear and supplies each porter carries. Since 1991, the Tanzanian government has required all hikers of Kilimanjaro to be accompanied by a licensed guide. The travel company that hosted our class, Trekking Hero, supported our group of 24 hikers with 11 guides and 53 porters. We quickly found ourselves reliant on the guides and porters for meals, setting up our tents, and making it to camp safely each day.

Our guides became much more than our leaders through the wilderness, though. As they hiked with us, they became our teachers, our best opportunity for understanding the culture of the people who live around Kilimanjaro. Our class had only one day to experience life in Moshi, the town at the base of Kilimanjaro, before beginning the climb. That day was spent on a safari in Arusha National Park.

We drove to the park in safari trucks through areas inhabited by the Maasai tribe, and caught glimpses out the open windows of people dressed in bright patterned robes, herding livestock with long sticks. The rest of the day was spent on *safari*, a Swahili word that, our driver proudly informed us, means "journey." We ventured through the national park in trucks and on foot, observing the graceful struts of giraffes and the antics of baboons. When we arrived back at Key's Lodge in Moshi, we started preparing for the six-day trek that began the next morning, without much discussion of the people who live around Kilimanjaro.

A focus on preparing for the hike, both physically and mentally, rather than on the cultural experience that lay before us left many students feeling curious. "This was such a once-in-a-lifetime experience that I would not trade for the world," Tim Boles, class of '20, said. "Being able to climb this mountain alongside the guides and porters was such an impactful experience. With that said, these connections we made on the mountain did not extend into our time in Moshi.

At times it felt as though we were there purely to climb Kilimanjaro and not to learn about all the wonderful aspects of Tanzanian culture and people."

Luckily, we were able to have plenty of conversations with the guides and porters during our climb. On the hour-long bus ride to the Machame Gate, the starting point for our climb, we sat next to Julius, the head guide from Trekking Hero. We discussed how Tanzania, formerly known as Tanganyika, gained its independence from the UK in 1961. At this time, Swahili became the official language of the country, which is inhabited by more than 125 different tribes, each with their own language.

Over the next six days, we learned about our guides' backgrounds and families, where they came from and who they were. We heard stories of banana beer shared with relatives at Christmas time, a farm owned and operated by a guide and his eight siblings, and pick-up soccer games in Moshi. We learned how our guides had worked as porters, how they had learned the flora and fauna of the five different ecosystems on the mountain, and how they had become experts in identifying the symptoms of altitude sickness, all during training to become guides.

Our guides were equally curious about our lives and asked us about our families, what we were studying, and what we wanted to do with our futures. "The guides and porters made an effort to get to know us individually, in addition to all of their other responsibilities," Nik Streit, class of '20, said. "They were very curious about our culture and were eager to tell us about their own." The guides and porters, with their stories, songs, and strength, propelled us through the first four days of hiking as much as our own determination and ability. Everyone in our group of 24 made it to Barafu High Camp.

Daniela expressing the mental and physical toll
of the mountain to our porters.
Courtesy of the Tanzania Wilderness and Adventure Course

"There was one day when I was really struggling to keep walking," said Daniela Nasser, class of '20. "A guide decided to go right in front of me and set a very slow pace. I felt safe following in his footsteps. When I could speak again, we talked about how the physical mountain and the mental mountain are separate things. He helped me realize that it's my job to carry myself mentally rather than physically."

After sleeping from 7 to 11 p.m. at Barafu High Camp, we started the climb to the highest point in Africa around midnight. One guide, Dennis, shared why the climb to the top starts at midnight: "Part of the reason is so that you can get to the top to see the sun rise. And part of the reason is because the weather isn't good during the afternoon, so we have to get up there and get back. And part of the reason is psychological, so that you can't see where you're going."

The guides, yet again, were what kept us moving. We rested every hour on the way up, but only for a few minutes at a time; it is important to keep moving due to the cold weather and the altitude. This pace is much more regulated than on the other days, when we walked at our own speed and our group of 25 slowly separated, a few guides to each clump of climbers. Summit Night is different: six hours of hiking up steep terrain in a single-file line, an ant trail of headlamps leading the way to the peak. Just after sunrise, we made it to Stella Point, the second-highest point on Kilimanjaro. Above the clouds, the view is breathtaking, quite literally.

"Stella Point felt like a breath of fresh air," Konnor Porro, class of '20, said. "After all of the planning, nerves, travel, and so on, I was finally where I hoped to be." We enjoyed the sunrise and rested for about 10 minutes before hiking the last hour to the highest point in Africa, Uhuru Peak. Our seasoned guides even carried some of our day packs to lessen the load. Some students had their packs taken by a guide during the six-hour trek to Stella Point. Mine was taken from me on the last stretch to Uhuru.

The first of our group arrive at Stella Point just after
sunrise after a long night of hiking.
Courtesy of the Tanzania Wilderness and Adventure Course

"Nothing lives up here. We have to move faster," said Godfrey, a guide who had been hiking with me since midnight. It was nearing 7 a.m. Godfrey took my pack and I made it—at a snail's pace—to Uhuru Peak. I was at Africa's highest point for less than 10 minutes, and my headache from the altitude made this time difficult to enjoy.

Another hour around the rim of the crater to reach
Uhuru Peak—Swahili for "Freedom."
Courtesy of the Tanzania Wilderness and Adventure Course

I had a day and a half of hiking to reflect on making the difficult climb to be at the top for mere minutes. As I walked through the rainforest, with enough distance from other hikers to feel alone with my thoughts, I realized how much more valuable the adventure had been to me than the peak. I reflected on how the guides had told me their life stories, and I began wondering how my experience on Kilimanjaro would weave into my own life story.

After a celebration dinner and the presentation of certificates certifying our climb from the Tanzania National Parks Association, we said goodbye to our guides, with promises to return to Tanzania. I friended Godfrey on Facebook so we could stay in touch. We had a few days in Tanzania after descending, which we filled with a trip to the Kikuletwa Hot Springs, a walking tour of Moshi, and a tour of a coffee farm nestled in the rainforest on the lower slopes of Kilimanjaro. We learned how to harvest, shell, and roast coffee beans in the tradition of the Chagga people. And we sampled some of the coffee—easily the best coffee I've ever had—before leaving for Kilimanjaro International Airport that afternoon and flying home.

Our fears at the beginning of the class had been fears of the unknown. Will I be able to summit? Will I get sick? Will I be injured? Some of our fears came true, but a broken ankle and two cases of altitude sickness later, the class persevered through the uncertainty and blazed a trail for "round two" of Elon-takes-Kilimanjaro in January 2021. "By the end of the trip, I found out that there was a lot to be afraid of, but I realized I didn't necessarily need to be fearful. Climbing Kilimanjaro taught me to be brave," Burke said.

I realized that my own fears had been misplaced; I had been most afraid that I wouldn't be able to summit Kilimanjaro. But the stories I heard, the people I met, and the Swahili songs I sang along the way form the memories I treasure from my time in Tanzania. "The peak made me realize the trip was about more than summiting," Porro said. "It was about forming friendships. Learning and experiencing Tanzanian culture. There were highs and there were lows, but the people on the trip had each other's backs the whole way through. Things do not always go to plan when you are 19,000 feet above sea level, but I could not have pictured the climb going any other way. The trip's imperfections are what made it one of the best experiences in my life."

Thinking back, I can hardly even remember Uhuru Peak. And although this memory lapse was probably the result of the altitude and lack of oxygen, my conviction stands: it is the *safari*—the journey—that matters most.

References

Adams, M., Bell, L. A., & Griffin, P. (Eds.). (1997). *Teaching for diversity and social justice: A sourcebook*. New York, Routledge.

Association for Experiential Education. (n.d.a). *Experiential education: The principles of practice* [Online]. Available at https://www.aee.org/what-is-ee (Accessed 1 July 2021).

Association for Experiential Education. (n.d.b). *What is experiential education?* [Online]. Available at http://www.aee.org/what-is-ee (Accessed 1 July 2021).

Beard, C. (2018, Summer). Dewey in the world of experiential education. *New Directions for Adult and Continuing Education*, *158*, 27–37 [Online]. Available at doi: 10.1002/ace.20276 27 (Accessed 23 February 2021).

Cason, D., & Gillis, H. L. (1994). A meta-analysis of outdoor adventure programming with adolescents. *Journal of Experiential Education*, *17*, 40–7.

Cullen, N. J., Sirguey, P., Mölg, T., Kaser, G., Winkler, M., & Fitzsimons, S. (2013). A century of ice retreat on Kilimanjaro: The mapping reloaded. *The Cryosphere*, *7*(2), 419–31 [Online]. Available at https://doi.org/10.5194/tc-7-419-2013 (Accessed 21 2021).

Dangi, T. B., & Jamal, T. (2016). An integrated approach to "Sustainable Community-Based Tourism." *Sustainability*, *8*(5), 475.

Daumal, R. (2004). *Mt. Analogue*. New York, Overlook Press.

Dausen, N. (2019). "Tanzania plans cable car for Mt. Kilimanjaro." Reuters, 7 May [Online]. Available at https://www.reuters.com/article/us-tanzania-tourism/tanzania-plans-cable-car-for-mount-kilimanjaro-idUSKCN1SD1OB (Accessed 20 January 2021).

Dewey, J. (1972). *The early works of John Dewey, 1882–1898* (vol. 5, 1895–1898). Carbondale, IL, Southern Illinois University Press.

Duckworth, A. L., Peterson, C., Matthews, M. D., & Kelly, D. R. (2007). Grit: Perseverance and passion for long-term goals. *Journal of Personality and Social Psychology, 92*(6), 1087–1101.

Garrison, D. R. (2007). Online Community of Inquiry review: Social, cognitive and teaching presence issues. *Journal of Asynchronous Learning Networks, 11*(1), 61–72.

Gillis, H. L., & Speelman, E. (2008). Are challenge (ropes) courses an effective tool? A meta-analysis. *Journal of Experiential Education, 31,* 111–35.

Goodman, J., & Kuzmic, J. (1997). Bringing a progressive pedagogy to conventional schools: Theoretical and practical implications from Harmony. *Theory Into Practice, 36*(2), 79–86.

Hans, T. (2000). A meta-analysis of the effects of adventure programming on locus of control. *Journal of Contemporary Psychotherapy, 30,* 33–60.

Hattie, J., Marsh, H. W., Neill, J. T., & Richards, G. E. (1997). Adventure education and Outward Bound: Out-of-class experiences that make a lasting difference. *Review of Educational Research, 67*(1), 43–87.

Johnson, A. (Ed.). (2006). *Power, privilege, and difference* (2nd ed.). New York, McGraw Hill Education.

Kilimanjaro Porters Assistance Project (KPAP). (n.d.). *What we do* [Online]. Available at https://kiliporters.org/what-we-do/ (Accessed 13 March 2021).

KiliSummit2001. (n.d.). *Geocaching: GC29PKY Kilimanjaro glacial sublimation* [Online]. Available at https://www.geocaching.com/geocache/GC29PKY_kilimanjaro-glacial-sublimation?guid=9decb0cd-43c0-4cd4-8ae2-c60cbad19fe81 (Accessed 21 March 2021).

Kolb, A. Y., & Kolb, D. A. (2017). *The experiential educator: Principles and practices of experiential learning.* Kaunakakai, HI, EBLS Press.

Kumashiro, K. (2015). *Against common sense: Teaching and learning toward social justice* (2nd ed.). New York, Routledge.

Levin, C. (n.d.). Only a teacher [Television broadcast]. (Accessed 17 September 2020).

Mtapuri, O., & Giampiccoli, A. (2019). Tourism, community-based tourism and ecotourism: A definitional problematic. *South African Geographical Journal, 101*(1), 22–35 [Online]. Available at https://doi.org/10.1080/03736245.2018.1522598 (Accessed 13 June 2021).

Mt. Kilimanjaro Guide. (n.d.). *When is the best time to climb Kilimanjaro?* [Online]. Available at https://www.mountkilimanjaroguide.com/kilimanjaro-weather.html (Accessed 3 July 2021).

Nelson, M. (2010, February 19). *Ten interesting facts about Mt. Kilimanjaro* [Online]. World Wildlife Foundation. Available at https://www.worldwildlife.org/blogs/good-nature-travel/posts/ten-interesting-facts-about-mt-kilimanjaro (Accessed 3 July 2021).

Peak Planet. (2019, March 14). *Who were the first people to climb Kilimanjaro?* [Online]. Available at https://peakplanet.com/who-were-the-first-people-to-climb-kilimanjaro (Accessed 1 August 2021).

Schuler, D. (2020, July 26). *Redefining ready—Will COVID-19 inspire educators to better prepare students for an uncertain future?* [Online]. Available at https://www.the74million.org/article/schuler-redefining-ready-will-covid-19-inspire-educators-to-better-prepare-students-for-an-uncertain-future/ (Accessed 9 December 2020).

Secret Compass. (n.d.). *The geography people and mythology of Africa's highest peak: What do you know about Kilimanjaro?* [Online]. Available at https://secretcompass.com/history-of-kilimanjaro (Accessed 13 December 2020).

Spring, J. (2018). *The American school: From the Puritans to the Trump era* (10th ed.). New York, Routledge.

Sterling, S. (2010). Learning for resilience, or the resilient learner? Towards a necessary reconciliation in a paradigm of sustainable education. *Environmental Education Research*, *15*, 511–28.

Strobl, A., Teichmann, K., & Peters, M. (2015). Do mountain tourists demand ecotourism? Examining moderating influences in an Alpine tourism context. *Tourism*, *62*(3), 383–98.

Wilson, S. J., & Lipsey, M. W. (2000). Wilderness challenge programs for delinquent youth: A meta-analysis of outcome evaluations. *Evaluation and Program Planning*, *23*(1), 1–12.

World Population Review. (n.d.). *GDP Ranked by Country 2020* [Online]. Available at https://worldpopulationreview.com/countries/countries-by-gdp (Accessed 20 January 2021).

Kilimanjaro Trekking Resources

Originally compiled by Tim Ward
Zombies on Kilimanjaro (Changemakers Books, 2012); used with permission

This section lists valuable information for anyone seeking to climb Mt. Kilimanjaro, beginning with some great organizations dedicated to the welfare of the porters, people, and environment. In particular, I recommend checking out the website of the Kilimanjaro Porters Assistance Project for a list of partner companies that adhere to their standards for the fair and ethical treatment of porters.

I also urge those interested in climbing Kilimanjaro to read the International Climbing and Mountaineering Federation (UIAA) Medical Commission brochure on travel at high altitude—the triple-starred reference below, which has crucial information on acute mountain sickness (AMS). I can't express strongly enough how important it is to familiarize yourself well with the dangers of altitude sickness before climbing Kilimanjaro, and to select a company that you have confidence can handle an emergency. People die every year climbing Kilimanjaro. The odds are remote, but they are real. Josh, Tim Ward's son, and I were fortunate. I was nowhere near as knowledgeable about AMS as I should have been, and since our climb, I have heard a few very sad stories.

Kilimanjaro Porters Assistance Project

Those who have climbed Mt. Kilimanjaro know that the porters are the heart and soul of the trek. Without their hard work and strength, climbers would not be able to fully experience the magnificence of Kilimanjaro. Porters are often impoverished Tanzanians who depend on this labor-intensive employment in order to feed themselves and their families. Porters can be underpaid and many climb without adequate clothing, footwear, or equipment. Porters are susceptible to altitude sickness, hypothermia and even death.

The Kilimanjaro Porters Assistance Project (KPAP) recognizes the value of the demanding labor these porters perform. Registered in January 2003, KPAP has been helping to improve the working conditions of the porters. Whether you are a climber, porter, guide, or managing a tour company, the Kilimanjaro Porters Assistance Project needs your help in ensuring fair treatment of all porters.

For more information please visit: http://www.kiliporters.org

International Mountain Explorers Connection

The International Mountain Explorers Connection (IMEC) is a U.S. 501(c)3 nonprofit organization founded in 1996 to promote responsible and sustainable connections between travelers and the people of developing mountain regions of the world. IMEC has a dual approach: working to benefit the local populations, primarily focusing on porters, while also working to educate visitors and link them to ways they can assist the local populations, particularly in demanding fair treatment for porters.

The International Mountain Explorers Connection created the Partnership for Responsible Travel Program to recognize those tour operators committed to fair treatment of the mountain crew. Acceptance as a Partner is based upon the climbing company's meeting IMEC's Guidelines for Proper Porter Treatment on Kilimanjaro through the monitoring activities performed by IMEC's local initiative, the Kilimanjaro Porters Assistance Project (KPAP).

For more information please visit: https://mountainexplorers. org/partnership-for-responsible-travel/

Medical Commission of the International Mountaineering and Climbing Federation (UIAA)

The UIAA's medical commission provides a medical information service for mountaineers, including a page on medical risks associated with climbing Kilimanjaro and visiting Tanzania. Their purpose is to give mountaineers reliable, practical advice and the most up to date recommendations on medical issues in the mountains. They function as a world-wide forum of doctors who are specialized in the different fields of mountain medicine. They collect, evaluate and discuss medical data from experts around the world and try to reach an international consensus on difficult issues of prevention and treatment of illness and injuries. They regularly publish recommendation papers which are available to everybody on the UIAA webpage. The UIAA's research includes issues of mountain equipment safety, diseases and altitude sickness, as well as Climate Change, sustainable development and supporting mountain cultures around the world.

www.theuiaa.org
www.theuiaa.org/kilimanjaro.html
https://www.theuiaa.org/mountain-medicine/
***https://www.theuiaa.org/mountain-medicine/travel-at-high-altitude-booklet-by-medex-a-must-read-for-adventurers/

Diamox: National Institutes of Health (NIH)
NIH has a valuable page on Diamox. Please research your

options well for preparing for altitude sickness.

https://www.ncbi.nlm.nih.gov
https://www.ncbi.nlm.nih.gov/pmc/
https://www.ncbi.nlm.nih.gov/pmc/articles/PMC2907615/
https://www.ncbi.nlm.nih.gov/pmc/?term=diamox

General Trekking Information on Kilimanjaro:

Mt. Kilimanjaro National Park
The Kilimanjaro page on the Government of Tanzania's Parks website has good basic information, maps, and lots of useful links about the country. For more information: www.tanzaniaparks.com/kili

KiliTrekker.com
Blog that invites anyone to post their experiences and recommendations on Kilimanjaro. For more information: http://kilitrekker.com

Kilimanjaro Climbs
Information on climbing Kilimanjaro (sponsored by a company, but with great general information). For more information: www.Kilimanjaroclimbs.com

Mt. Kilimanjaro Travel Guide
Information website for climbing Kilimanjaro. For more information: www.mtkilimanjarologue.com

TripAdvisor: Kilimanjaro National Park
Reviews and recommendations from trekkers who have climbed Kilimanjaro. For more information: www.tripadvisor.com/Tourism-g293750-Kilimanjaro_National_Park-Vacations

**CHANGEMAKERS
BOOKS**

TRANSFORMATION

Transform your life, transform your world - Changemakers Books
publishes books for individuals committed to transforming their
lives and transforming the world. Our readers seek to become
positive, powerful agents of change. Changemakers Books inform,
inspire, and provide practical wisdom and skills to empower us
to write the next chapter of humanity's future.

Zombies on Kilimanjaro
A Father/Son Journey Above the Clouds
Tim Ward
On a journey to the roof of Africa, a father and son traverse the treacherous terrain of fatherhood, divorce, dark secrets and old grudges, and forge an authentic new relationship.
Paperback 978-1-78099-339-3; e-book: 978-1-78099-340-9

How to Lead a Badass Business From Your Heart
The Permission You've Been Waiting for to Birth Your Vision and Spread Your Glitter in the World
Makenzie Marzluff
A blueprint for conscious young entrepreneurs to bring their business to life in a way that is entirely rooted in the heart. While the old paradigm of business was rooted in fear and greed, this book grants full permission to visionaries to restore heart on our planet through their creations.
Paperback 978-1-78904-636-6; e-book: 978-1-78904-637-3

Everything You Never Learned About Sex
Take Back Your Masculine Power & Use Your Sex Energy For Good
Michael McPherson
Michael McPherson shines a light on what it was like for the men of his millennial generation to mature sexually, and why so many still haven't.
Paperback 978-1-78904-638-0; e-book 978-1-78904-639-7

Resilience Series

The Resilience Series is a collaborative effort by the authors of Changemakers Books in response to the 2020-21 coronavirus epidemic. Each concise volume offers expert advice and practical exercises for mastering specific skills and abilities. Our intention is that by strengthening your resilience, you can better survive and even thrive in a time of crisis.

www.resilience-books.com

Resetting Our Future Series

At this critical moment of history, with a pandemic raging, we have the rare opportunity for a Great Reset – to choose a different future. This series provides a platform for pragmatic thought leaders to share their vision for change based on their deep expertise. For communities and nations struggling to cope with the crisis, these books will provide a burst of hope and energy to help us take the first difficult steps towards a better future.

www.resettingourfuture.com